SPARK

Igniting Your Dreams

DR. GREG AYERS

TESTIMONIALS FOR
DR. GREG AYERS AND SPARK

Having known Dr. Ayers for over 20 years, I have watched his Dental practice transition to powerhouse success.

What I have recognized is that it stems from his immense integrity his compassion for the people he serves and works with. His passion for the work he does is contagious and extends to each member of his 100 + team.

He is an intentional leader, meaning he is very much aware of what it takes to lead and inspire others to greatness, and he works at this consciously.

His success happens to be showcased in his dental practice. However, he would shine in any business entity. The principles in this book can be translated into any business from the new entrepreneur to the global organization.

Having worked with leaders for the past 15 years from all levels of the organization from entry level to C- Suite, across the country and globe, this book is a must read for everyone. There is something to learn or remember for all leaders.

- Elizabeth Jende Chevalier, President, EJC Move Consulting

Dr. Ayers work within the dental industry has been nothing short of extraordinary. He is a thought leader and has the unique ability of distilling down information to the most important points. I am excited for this book to give some guidance from his experience and leadership skills to the dental community. There are books, and then there are those that will speak to you. This will speak to you! DO NOT MISS IT!!!

- Dee Fischer, CEO & Founder of Fischer Professional Group

Good customer experiences don't happen by accident. They start with the mindset of cultivating relationships and Dr. Greg Ayers shows you how it's done in this quick-yet-valuable read. Plus, he shows you how to get your team on board so you all succeed together. I've experienced Dr. Ayer's business first-hand and what he teaches in this book works!

- Maureen Perideaux, Copywriter and Creativity Speaker

Dr. Ayers, or Greg, as I like to call him is the truest form of "Walking the Walk." Through all his adversities he has never once wavered from his faith in God and his commitment to always doing for others. He continues to be my inspiration and I am honored to call him my friend.

- Jacleen Haber, Actress/Model

Greg Ayer's passion for life is contagious. I first met him when he and his family joined the church I served as pastor. Shortly thereafter, he became my dentist and dear friend.

Greg possesses the greatest quality needed to be successful in any business - he genuinely cares about people. While he is an extraordinary, innovative dentist, he is even more adept at building lasting relationships.

Greg is never satisfied! Good enough, is never good enough with him. He is always looking to find ways to make his practice more conducive to the needs of his patients.

What perhaps, is even more amazing, is that he has both cast a vision for his staff and effectively trained them to bring his dream to fruition. That isn't easily done! But they have hit it out of the park.

If you are looking for a coach or a mentor who can help you ignite your dreams, Dr. Greg Ayers is your man.

- Dr. Ralph F. Carter

My friend and colleague, Dr Greg Ayers not only talks the talk, but walks the walk!

Success, as Greg points out, is having a positive attitude and a matching positive mindset. What we put into the Universe comes back in spades. Great relationships equal monetary as well as emotional success.

Allow the words within Greg's book to inspire each of you to remember that "positive outlooks create positive outcomes."

- Linda Miles, Speaker, Consultant, Author

Dr. Greg Ayers/Spark
Printed in the United States of America

Spark/ Dr. Greg Ayers -- 1st ed.

ISBN 9798390507568 Print Edition

CONTENTS

This book is dedicated to my sons Chad, Blake, Brent, and Chandler who inspire me with their Spark and entrepreneur spirit.

OTHER BOOKS BY DR. GREG AYERS

The Service Prescription:
Healthcare The Way It Was Meant To Be

"Your dreams are the blueprint of reality."
–Greg Norman, PGA professional golfer

INTRODUCTION

In *Spark: Igniting Your Dreams*, Dr. Greg Ayers takes you on a quest to live the fullest life possible by understanding the true meaning of success. In life, success has everything to do with the relationships we cultivate. In business, success is not about the product or service we sell but rather about the experience we deliver to each and every customer, each and every client, each and every person who walks through our doors. It's about doing the big things well and executing the small details superbly, both in life and business.

Spark: Igniting Your Dreams will inspire you to launch your dreams and desires and to become incredibly passionate about delivering an exceptional experience to the people in your life and to your customers every single day your door opens for business, regardless of your industry.

If there is a formula to follow, it is this: Life is a matter of mindset. It is the one thing we can control. Mindset is what you decide it can be. It dictates your dreams, your focus, and your determination. If you refuse to give up, you'll never have to look back on your life or career with regret. We are all seeking the spark necessary to ignite our dreams, and the answers lie within the pages of this book.

CHAPTER ONE

UNCLE FRED AND THE
EXCEPTIONAL EXPERIENCE

In early 2012, I remember waking up, staring at the ceiling, and wondering, "What am I gonna do now?"

For the first time in years, I didn't know. Three decades before, I had started a dental practice in a tiny cracker-box house, which I liked to say was located "five miles from nowhere." We eventually ended up with one of the largest dental practices in South Carolina. Our growth wasn't by accident. I built my business by first considering, "What can we do, as a dental team, every day, in every encounter, to make our patients feel valued?"

I encourage you to ask the same question. Just insert the word customer or end user of the product or services you provide. The result we achieved was like igniting a rocket. For the next 29 years, I was intently focused on giving our patients an exceptional experience, and they rewarded me with an exceptionally happy and successful career. Life as I knew it was pretty much on autopilot.

Then, in the twinkling of an eye, I came to a roadblock. Yes, bumps in the road do occur, even though everything appears fine around you. As the practice expanded, I took on more partners, and the company grew to multiple dental locations, and it became impossible to keep my company's original vision and mission intact. Just like cooking a live lobster by slowly turning up the heat, I saw my vision slowly eroding. In the last few years, I wasn't waking up eager to get to work anymore. For a guy who is enthusiastic and optimistic by nature, my ebbing enthusiasm for the business I built from scratch next to a cow field was a sign that I needed to change things. I knew it was time to cut my business ties and move on. It was, without question, the most difficult decision I've ever had to make.

So, in 2011, I resigned as the senior partner of the practice I founded and faced the fact that I was in a very unusual place for me—staring into the unknown. I knew this much: I didn't believe I had the energy or desire to start my career over again. "I'm just gonna hang it up. My family and I are doing fine. I don't need to start over. I'm not gonna go through this again at this stage in my life."

After many late-night discussions and prayers with my family, they concluded that it was never too late to reignite your dreams. Two of our sons, Brent and Blake, were just finishing college, and they came to me expressing an interest in pursuing a career in the dental business. I vividly remember the conversation. They were like two thoroughbreds ready to bolt from the starting gate.

"Let's dream BIG, Dad!" Let's take what you've successfully created over the past 29 years and take it to a much higher level! Like "dentistry reimagined." They wanted to do something special together. Their inspiration reignited my passion and dream to step up to the plate and get back into the game.

Blake entered the dental sales side of our business, and Brent set his sights on running and managing dental offices. It inspired me to see their energy and passion to jump out of the boat into unchartered waters and together pursue a goal.

Their enthusiasm started to bring back mine. Looking at the future through their fresh perspective, I realized that we could build a new practice on the foundation of delivering a product I called "service excellence," and this time, we could show others, regardless of their profession or their industry of choice, how they could do it, too.

Yes, trials and tribulations, setbacks, and heartaches do come for everyone, no matter their circumstances. What I can tell you, however, is that **when the storms of life come, and darkness is all around you, the sun always comes up the next day!**

I realized that it doesn't matter what profession you're in; the principles of building success apply whether your job is dentistry or building a hot dog business. Now, I spent my entire professional career restoring teeth and creating beautiful smiles. I have very little experience on how to cook a killer hot dog but give me a hot dog stand and 90 days, and I feel confident we could have one of the most successful hot dog stands around. The success of your company isn't just related to the *product* you make or the service you provide. The measure of success rather comes from the *experience* your customer receives when you and your team deliver it!

———

**Success is not about the product or service.
Success is about the experience you deliver to each and
every customer, each and every client, each and every
person who walks through your door.**

———

This book is meant to inspire you to launch your dreams and desires and to become incredibly passionate about delivering an exceptional experience to your customers every single day your door opens for business, regardless of your industry. The age-old axiom that says, "If you love what you do, you'll never have to work another day in your life," is true in every sense of the word.

***

Thanks for investing your time in allowing me to share with you a blueprint meant to create the spark necessary to ignite your dreams. I've spent most of my career studying and observing why some companies succeed and why others fail. Often, these companies even manufacture the same product.

Why do some businesses soar with the eagles, and others just accept being average?

Great businesses don't just do the big things well; they execute the small details superbly!

ACHIEVING EXCELLENCE

Great businesses just don't do the big things well; they execute the small details superbly! Achieving excellence isn't just one thing: it's many things done exceptionally well.

You might not have the wisdom or 30+ years of experience in your profession, but there are ways to gain wisdom more quickly. As

I reflect on my life, I realize there were several critical moments in time that shaped my life and career. None of these were more powerful than having great mentors to guide me and keep me focused on what was important. I like to refer to mentors as "banks along the river" as you go through life.

When the river runs smoothly, life is good and all is well, running without a hitch downstream. But when storms are brewing, and the waters are rising, floods will come, and turbulent water will overflow the banks. With that storm, uncertainty comes, doubts arise, and you begin to question if you are even on the correct path. Often, we're tempted to throw in the towel. That's where great mentors shine! They help you navigate during these difficult times, knowing that the rising waters always recede and the banks will slowly steer you back on course. The most highly successful individuals I know have a similar story they can share and relate with you.

Achieving excellence also covers every aspect of life, from the people you hire and how you train them to figuring out your personal goals and sticking to them, no matter what's thrown at you.

I've learned that whether you are creating a company strategy or figuring out your own next step as an individual, goals are easy to talk about but often hard to carry out. You need mentors to help you stay focused on what's important. Just because something is important doesn't mean it's always clear.

At some point, every one of us reaches what seems to be a crossroads in life where we're not sure what direction we should take. I like to use the image of a "Y" for the this-way-or-that-way points in life. Depending on the branch you take, you can either be veered away from your goal, or you can continue to press forward with your dream. Many times when we are stuck, trying to discern which direction to take, we are persuaded to follow the crowd, taking the easy path instead of the road less traveled. For a young person, it could be as simple as a decision about how to spend Friday night. Will it be spent being pressured by your peers to try the latest drug for the first time or finish that college application? This "Y"—which you can also interpret as "Why?!"—is the critical point, and we all have them. "Why go this way or that way?"

That's when mentors step in. I believe mentors are critical to success since they keep you focused on your goals during the dark times, the times when you can't tell which path to choose or when circumstances seem hopeless. You need help in those times.

I've been blessed with amazing mentors who kept me focused and who will be a part of this book—mentors like Jack Bogart, one of my first patients, who was one of the original artists for Walt Disney, and Og Mandino, who rose from homelessness to become one of the most successful motivational speakers and writers in the world. John Maxwell who is known for his outstanding corporate leadership skills. Then there's T. Scott Gross, an inspiring writer and nationally renowned keynote speaker to corporate America, who I met in a surprising way and who became the co-author of my first book, *The Service Prescription: Healthcare the Way It Was Meant to Be.*

These mentors and many others have been invaluable to me. But before they came into my life, there was Uncle Fred.

***

I had my career's first aha moment because of my wife's Uncle Fred. I began dating my wife at age 19 and was fascinated from the very beginning with Uncle Fred and what he did to build his amazingly successful company. He inspired me to **not only dream big, but to dream smart**. His unusual route to success was only possible because he knew how to take a dream, turn it into a goal, and follow that goal to exactly where he wanted to go.

Uncle Fred started out as a cop in the late 50s. In the early 60s, with a wife and four small kids, Uncle Fred took a leap of faith and resigned from his job as a police officer (making a whopping $3,200 per year), packed up his family and all his belongings, and moved to Tallahassee, Florida. As it turned out, Uncle Fred was listening to another kind of siren, the siren call to become an entrepreneur and open his own beauty supply business—or, as he likes to say, "Selling bobby pins and shampoo out of the trunk of my car." Fast forward some 20 years, and Uncle Fred was the proud owner of one of the most successful privately held beauty supply companies in America.

Why was Uncle Fred successful? Not because he sold more bobby pins or a better shampoo product, but because the main product he was selling was wrapped up and presented to his customers every single time he entered their place of business in what he termed "service excellence." I remember him telling me how well-trained his employees were. When they went out on a sales call, they greeted every person by name as if they were best friends. They knew everyone's birthday and how many kids they had. On special occasions, they showed up with flowers. If you didn't know better, you might assume that Uncle Fred's salesforce existed for the sole purpose of making each business owner and his or her staff happy. In fact, that *was* the goal. Uncle Fred didn't merely provide each client with beauty supplies—any beauty supply company can do that—but he offered each client the best service experience ever. Period!

While I was in college, dreaming about what I wanted to do, Uncle Fred's lessons stayed with me. I was enamored with his values. He believed in building lasting relationships with people and treating every customer as if his company's success depended on it. No matter the setback or obstacle, Uncle Fred kept his eye fixed on his goals. He was never afraid to dream beyond his present circumstances or become unduly discouraged when faced with challenges.

IT FACTOR

Learning the art of goal setting and goal keeping brought me the fruits of success, too. It also steadied me through some very painful low points in my life. Uncle Fred was one of my first mentors to impress on me this one guiding principle: **Goals are met by building excellence from even the smallest details**.

If you're thinking, "Sure, everyone has goals—what's so unusual about that?" you're right. Everyone has some type of dream that has them saying, "I'd love to do this. I'd love to do that." But how many are persistent enough to take the next step?

I often pondered this very fascinating question: What is it that separates two people who graduated from the same college with the same degree, with equally impressive grades and similar study habits? Two individuals who had similarly passionate goals? Yet five years later, one of them is on the list of "The Best Entrepreneurs Under Thirty," while the other is struggling just to stay in business.

That question has always intrigued me. What separates the exceptional from the ordinary? What makes one individual or company great and another individual or company that sells the same product or service merely average? Is it good looks, IQ, or money? Oh, did I happen to mention that Uncle Fred had a sixth-grade education and was the oldest of eight children, and his father was a Baptist preacher in a tiny mill village?

Years later, it took my sons grabbing me by the shoulders, swinging me around, and saying, "Dad, you answered that question with your first successful business!"

It was true. When you create a unique, exceptional experience for your patients or customers, they also answer that same question. How? They keep coming back. Even more amazingly, they refer their family, friends, and co-workers to your business.

––––––

Today, the tagline for our company is: "Creating the Perfect Patient Experience."

––––––

As I often remind our team, "We're not here to sell a crown or a root canal or a dental implant or a teeth cleaning. We're all here to sell a product called Service Excellence."

Let's face it: When it comes to delivering a fun-loving experience, I chose a profession that's a hard sell. Dentistry is usually not on most individuals' top ten list of things they want to experience in life! A dental appointment isn't exactly the first choice for people who are in search of a good time. It's not like going to a movie, or a theme park or even shopping for a new car. You walk in the door with, at best, average expectations. So, to make people happy to go to the dentist—to give them what we call the Perfect Patient Experience (PPE)—is pretty much ultimate proof that the qualities that made Uncle Fred successful can be applied to every person and in any business.

BORN AN ENTREPRENEUR

Was I an unusual kid growing up in a small farm town in Indiana? Maybe. I remember being five or six years old and sitting in the sandbox in the backyard, thinking, "I wonder what I could invent?" I always wanted to do something special. It's like my brain was wired to crackle with ideas and questions such as "What if I made something that nobody ever saw before?" and "What if I do something when I grow up that is really special?"

Questions like that energized me throughout school. Our little elementary school had a student newspaper. When I was in the fifth grade, I was interviewed for a story, and they asked me this question: "What do you want to be when you grow up?" I said, "I want to be a professional golfer, and I want to be a dentist." How's that for covering both ends of the career spectrum! Oh, by the way, I hated going to the dentist!

Well, OK, golf pro or dentist? It wasn't as if I had an inside track to do either. I was the furthest thing from a kid born with a silver spoon in my mouth. My parents worked hard to provide for four children, and it was up to me to finance my own education. But almost as soon as I started college, it looked like my money worries were over: This little ol' country boy from Indiana got a golf scholarship to attend a college in Florida.

Youthful arrogance caused me to assume I was set for life, and that's always a dangerous thing to do. When you start thinking like that, somehow, it gives life a poke in the eye, and she decides to show her cruel side. For me, it happened during my second year of college. I was coming back from a golf tournament when I was in a terrible car accident. Besides hitting the windshield, which was bad enough, I sustained a compound fracture of my femur, the largest bone in the body. Unfortunately for me, modern medicine hadn't perfected the technology they have today to insert a rod into your femur that allows patients with similar breaks to be up walking on crutches within a few days. Consequently, I was confined to a hospital bed in traction for two months while my femur was healing back together, and then plastered in a body cast from the chest down for six more months. I'm not sure if I really comprehended what they were doing or saying, but when I woke up in the recovery room flat on my back, totally immobilized and wrapped in hot plaster, I knew my life as I had originally planned was over.

After a two-month hiatus in the hospital in Florida and a 16-hour ambulance ride from Florida to my parents' house in Greenville, South Carolina, I vividly remember lying in the front room of a rented hospital bed, thinking to myself, "Man, my life and dreams are over. My golf career is done." That accident hadn't just crushed my leg; it crushed every dream and goal I had been working for at least since high school.

Today, I look back and realize that car accident that crushed my femur was one of the best things that ever happened to me. Without that car accident, I probably would have flunked out of school that year. I didn't take studying very seriously, and the kinds of courses

I was taking—such as organic chemistry, comparative anatomy, and physics—don't just float into your head like a piece of music. I was on the fast track to failure and didn't know it.

That accident also opened the door to one of the happiest, life-changing events there is. During my recuperation, I met my wife, Sharon, who was finishing up nursing school. Over the course of the next two years, the question almost every person faces at some point, "Who are you going to spend your life with?" was answered, and the new responsibilities of being married helped me get my head back on straight.

No sooner did I get that major event in place than my old dream-building machine kicked into my head again, and I said to myself, "Man, I wish I had another goal!"

That's when I went back to the second half of the dream I had had since the fifth grade: to be a dentist. Through newly matured eyes, I faced the fact that I wasn't going to be a professional golfer, but that didn't mean I couldn't love golf. As far as a profession went, it was time to buckle down, and I told myself, "I'm going after this journey called dentistry." Clearly, from the fifth grade, I had my major goals pretty much lined up—golf or dentistry—and I still have the newspaper story to prove it.

I was laser-focused on making the grades and shadowing as many dental practices that would let me in.

**Hardships and struggles can often help you refocus
your direction in life.
It sure did mine!**

I was accepted to the Medical University of South Carolina, College of Dental Medicine, in May of 1979, and I proudly graduated in May of 1983.

***

I opened my first practice in Greenville, South Carolina, in a little 1,000-square-foot house owned by my wife's aunt and uncle. I had exactly four patients, my in-laws and my parents, and the company of some cows over the next fence line. I remember thinking, "How do dentists build these huge successful dental practices? I'll never be able to do it."

Around that time, I recall driving down the interstate, probably five miles from my office when suddenly I caught sight of a billboard. The billboard was completely blank except for one sentence. Something about that sentence grabbed me so much that I thought, "What did that billboard just say?" and I literally got off at the next exit, turned around, and came back to read it again. It read:

"There's no heavier burden than a great opportunity." I stopped the car and stared at that sentence for the longest time. I thought of my little dental practice and my dreams of really making something of my life. I remember saying under my breath, over and over, "There is no heavier burden than a great opportunity" as I thought about all the dentists in my area; it felt almost like there was one on every corner. I wondered to myself, "How was I ever going to stand out from that crowd?" I was just a young whippersnapper who didn't know a thing about building and running a dental practice.

As I thought about it and drilled down a little further into the burdens I faced, it didn't look any better. "People hate going to the dentist! How do you overcome that?"

Then I started thinking about the second half of that sentence—"the great opportunity." The fact that people "hate" going to the dentist can be the best marketing tool of all. Everybody knows what to expect at the dentist's office, so why not give them the unexpected—the exceptional experience?

I was a young guy out of dental school, so it took time to figure out what that exceptional experience could be. You don't just wake up one day and say, "I want to be a professional baseball player," and go out and buy a baseball, glove, and bat, and that's it. I saw the opportunity, but I also saw the burden. I realized I would have to work hard, build slowly, and keep my eyes focused on my goal if I wanted to get someplace.

I thought of Uncle Fred building his business out of the trunk of his car, and I thought, "I've got a dream, I know where I want to go, and I don't care what it takes. I'm going to make it. I don't want to give up saying, 'This is too hard. I don't want to do this anymore.' Someday it's going to pay off."

Well, of course, it did pay off. I applied the principles that made Uncle Fred a success in delivering the exceptional experience. That was the launchpad that ignited my first dream and built my own first successful business.

Then in 2012, I began again by opening a new practice in Woodruff, South Carolina. This time, it was my son Brent who opened my eyes to the burden of the next great opportunity when he said, "OK, Dad, let's take this to the next level."

That's like throwing gas on the fire for me. I said, "Man, that's awesome, Brent. Let's go." It was also the love and support of my entire family that propelled us to light the fuse of our dreams.

We called our new practice ProGrin Dental. We concentrate one hundred percent on our entire team delivering the Perfect Patient Experience.

I think back and realize that if it wasn't for Uncle Fred and mentors like Jack Bogart and T. Scott Gross, I could easily still be in that first little house across from a cow pasture, the go-to guy for once-a-year checkups and cavity fillings, yet never fulfilling my dreams. Instead, I took all those tools that I was given by my mentors and my own experiences and used them to ignite my own dreams. Now, buckle up, as I'd like to show you how to launch yours.

CHAPTER TWO

THE TWO GREATEST WORDS IN THE ENGLISH LANGUAGE

At some point during their teenage years, I asked all my sons this question: "What are the two greatest words in the English language?" Of course, they looked back at me like deer in headlights. So, I put them out of their misery by exclaiming, "What If!"

"What If?" is the fuel that sparks great innovative ideas. It's the DNA of entrepreneurs. One, two, three people sitting around discussing a great idea, and one person interjects, "What if we were to…" You fill in the rest.

When the idea is laid out there, another person enthusiastically says, "What an awesome idea, but what if we took it to a higher level and did this?"

The third interjects by saying, "And we can take that idea and do this." Suddenly, a great idea has been exponentially transformed from a good idea to an amazing idea by playing the What-If? Game.

On the flip side, I will tell you that those two great thought-provoking words can also become the two most dejecting words in the English language. How sad to have shared your dream and great idea with your close friend or friends and never acted upon it!

———

To look back on that 25 years later and say, "Man...what if we had only followed through on our great idea?" Tragedy.

———

How sad to go through life always wondering what life would have looked like if only we would have acted on our What-If? Dream. It's just a matter of inflection...how you say it, the tone of your voice, "WHAT IF...?" vs. "what if..." sigh.

I get fired up when hanging around people who play the What-If? Game. I've done this with two or three people at a time. We sit down, lock ourselves in a room with cups of coffee, and just sit there. We might not talk for 20 minutes, maybe even longer. In the silence, we let those two words play around in our minds, conjuring up scenarios, plans, and dreams. Then we open up the throttle and let those two words fly into the air.

If there are three people in the room, you just don't get three times the ideas (3x); you get ideas X to the third power (X^3). You get exponential growth because now that you've got everyone thinking at a higher plane.

When entrepreneurs get together to say, "That's awesome. What if we did this to that?" the creative shrapnel starts flying in all directions. Sure, some of it's crazy and impractical, but eventually, there will be enough ideas left over that could change the course of a company or an individual.

Do you want to find the Spark that will ignite your dreams? Strap those two words together and see what happens. What If?

If you're an entrepreneur, the question can send your company in a new direction or launch a new brand: "What if we open a second location? What if I take on a partner?"

It works in families: "What if we sold the house? What if we decide to buckle up and commit to paying off our credit cards and live debt-free?"

On a personal level: "What if I apply for that job? What if I went back to college or took night classes? What if I take a chance and ask that person to go out with me?" There is no undertaking that doesn't benefit from taking time to play the What-If? Game.

Without realizing it, I started playing What If? in the sandbox when I was about five years old, and it kicked off a lifetime of goal setting. I asked myself, "What if I do something when I grow up that is really special?"

My first two dreams were audacious: "What if I became a golf pro or dentist? What if?!" Yes, I actually thought that as far back as I could remember.

One of the most important things I learned from my sandbox exercise was this: Even if the answer is no, the exercise is just as valuable. Sure, as a young boy, I grew up dreaming of the day I'd win the green jacket at the Masters Tournament and share the leaderboard with guys named Palmer and Nicklaus. When that door closed for me in the 1970s, I was still glad I had asked the question. Even if my golf dreams didn't bear fruit, they planted new seeds. They got me to college in Florida, set the course for meeting my wife, Sharon, and forced me to shape up and mature so I could buckle down to my second goal, which was dentistry. All of that triggered a whole new round of exciting What-If? Exercises.

While I'd like to think that I dreamed up the game in my sandbox, in fact, the What-If? Exercise has a long history. Companies use the question to enhance their strategic planning, mentors use it to inspire their clients, and spiritual leaders use it to prompt people to seek deeper meaning in their lives.

Author and journalist Warren Berger is known for his challenging insights that were first shared in an article titled "Unleashing the Power of Beautiful Questions." Berger considers What If? to be one of those key questions that every business—even every person—should be asking. In 2016, he wrote a guest column in *The New York Times* that starts with a question of his own. He was meeting with a chief executive who was worried about several of her senior managers, even though they were smart and experienced. "So, what was the problem?" Berger asked. "They're not asking enough questions," she said.

Berger makes the point that in the past, people were expected to know their job, stay quiet, and not bother management. Today, he writes, "I'm finding that business leaders want the people working around them to be more curious, more cognizant of what they don't know, and more inquisitive." In other words, asking questions that might lead to their companies discovering new and innovative new opportunities.

———

In today's best companies, employees aren't just expected to follow the rules; they are expected to participate in the success of the organization.

———

That means that even the newest, most inexperienced employee can change a company's direction by offering What Ifs? To fix problems, create new methods of doing business, and find new ways to implement and improve the perfect customer experience.

The fact is, there are no questions too small or too modest to ask, and there's no piece of paper too small to pick up from the floor. Everything matters when you are creating an exceptional experience. In his book, *A More Beautiful Question,* Warren Berger writes about the first instant-photo camera, the Land Camera, and what inspired its invention. It was invented in the 1940s thanks to an innocent question posed by a three-year-old child. As the story goes, the inventor, Edwin H. Land, was showing off his new camera to his daughter. Impatient to see the photo that her father had just snapped, she was even more frustrated when he explained the film had to be processed first. Her response was a thing of inspiration:

"Why do we have to *wait* for the picture?"

That child's question launched a brand and revolutionized an industry.

Mike Myatt, the bestselling author of *Hacking Leadership* and *Leadership Matters,* believes that, many times, the obstacles that stand in the way of unleashing success are actually pretty simple. "Change," he says, "doesn't need to be complex. In fact, what's simpler than using the filter of What If? It doesn't require any special skills or ability, just the willingness to look beyond what presently exists."

In other words, even a child can do it.

Myatt notes, "The process of unleashing What If? Begins with not painting yourself into corners."

"The single greatest barrier impeding the transition from What Is? to What If? is allowing yourself to fall into the trap of either/or thinking. The best leaders realize there's rarely a good reason to juxtapose one option against another."
-Mike Myatt

Looking back over my own professional life as a dentist and business owner, I recognize those times when I've allowed myself to be "painted into a corner." That's when it's time to break out, move forward, and ask a new fresh set of What-If? Questions. It's important to always be ready to think outside of the sandbox.

That doesn't mean abandoning everything you've done. As Mike Myatt points out, the best leaders stay focused on their desired outcomes, preserve what's good, stayed focused while remaining "discovery-driven." His point is to always be willing to step back periodically to discover what's new and what's ahead.

DISCOVERY DRIVEN

In 1992, I set myself up for a new, discovery-driven What-If? Question, which opened a whole new dimension to my life.

At that time, I had been in my first dental practice for nine years and really wanted to take my business to another new level of success. I was convinced that I had a lot to offer my profession, especially from the patient's perspective and to the business community. But what was the best way?

Early in my career, I felt much like a renegade in the dental community, and I was probably perceived as such by some of my colleagues. You've heard the saying: Don't upset the apple cart. Well, in many ways, I did.

Back then, I felt as if dentistry focused more on the needs and desires of the dentist and not so much on the most important person in our profession: the patient. I started exploring some business What-If? Scenarios. What if we began accepting assignment of dental insurance benefits where the patient would only have to pay a co-pay? That would relieve a lot of the financial burden on the patient. The patient would not have to pay for their entire procedure up front and then have to wait 2-3 weeks before their insurance reimbursed them. What if we altered our conventional office hours from the traditional 8-5 Monday through Thursday and offered extended hours beginning at 7 am, two days a week? What if the other two days of the week we offered evening hours until 7:00 p.m.? Then we could offer office hours every other Saturday. What If? Talk about throwing salt into an open wound!

So, that's what we did. And lo and behold, we were featured in a story in the local newspaper with a picture of me and Robin, my dental assistant, next to a patient in one of our dental chairs. The picture was taken in the evening as if the photographer were looking in through the office window. The article explained that we were offering expanded office hours to people who weren't able to come in during normal office hours.

Because of this simple What If?, the phones began ringing off the hook.

It was a game changer to assure patients that they would not have to pay out-of-pocket for, say, $400 for dental cleanings for their four children on a procedure that was reimbursed 100% twice a year.

The volume of patients wanting their dental records transferred from their previous dentist to ours was astronomical. No, it was never my intent to steal patients from other practices. This rush of new patients was simply the result of doing something for the patient that had never been done before.

The crazy thing is, within five or so years, most dentists were following suit by offering extended office hours and accepting assignment of dental insurance benefits like we were.

Let's be honest; too many businesses get "stuck" in their ways. They continue to do business under the auspices of "If it ain't broke, don't fix it."

I personally love those businesses because they make us stand out.

At ProGrin Dental, we prefer to say, "If it ain't broke, break it!"

———

Remember this, "If Nothing Ever CHANGES, Then Nothing ever Changes!"

———

Through my commitment to service excellence, the tiny practice I opened in 1983 next to a cow pasture exploded in growth. I knew

I was on to something, and I wanted to share it with others, but I didn't know the best way to do it.

Through a roundabout series of events and a willingness to ask myself, "What if I take this risk or that risk?" I expanded my reach in ways I never imagined.

It all began one day with a simple conversation over breakfast with my pastor, Dr. Ralph Carter, of Brushy Creek Baptist Church in Greenville, South Carolina. He and I were friends, and I also happened to be his dentist, so we often got wrapped in long, easygoing conversations about our lives.

Dr. Carter asked me this question, "Your office is unlike any other dental office I've ever been to. To what do you attribute the success and growth of your dental practice?" Dr. Carter pastored one of the largest churches in town, so coming from him, the question kind of set me back. I thanked him for the nice compliment and then shared my story and talked about how my mentors, Uncle Fred and Jack Bogart, guided me to where I am today. I explained how these non-dentists had instilled an ethic of service excellence in me.

Then I told Dr. Carter about a book I pulled off the shelf at Barnes and Noble in 1992 that essentially put into print everything Uncle Fred and Jack Bogart had coached me on for the past nine years. Published just the year before, it was titled *POS: Positively Outrageous Service.* The writer was a highly regarded business consultant and motivational speaker, T. Scott Gross.

Reading this book had reaffirmed in me classic business principles, but they were presented in such a fresh way that I found it exciting. I re-read *POS* so many times—each time with a different colored highlighter. After a while, the book looked like a package of

Skittles had melted inside of it. Gross's message was that businesses can set themselves apart and prosper by returning to a tried-and-true ingredient for success—but by using modern methods and ideas to get there.

Take the classic tenet of providing good customer service and ramp it up by providing Positively Outrageous Service, which is exceptional service that is above and beyond the call of duty.

I explained to Pastor Carter how I was using Scott Gross's business principles in my own practice. Well, I must have been pretty inspiring because the next thing you know, Pastor Carter went out and bought Scott's book and used it as the basis for three sermons. Then he wrote Scott a letter, enclosed copies of the recorded sermons on cassette, and wrote about the dentist (yours truly) who inspired him to learn the secrets of success through delivering POS.

A while later, Pastor Carter beckoned to me after church and said, "Scott Gross wrote me back to say how much he appreciated the fact that you recommended his book!" That got me thinking, "If Pastor Carter can write Scott a letter, why can't I? What if I wrote to him and told him how much he had influenced my own business and my life?"

So, I did just that. I intended to write a brief and polite note acknowledging Scott's role in inspiring me to build a world-class, customer-service-oriented business. When I was done, my tiny one-pager had expanded to nine and a half pages. On the last page, I left my new mentor with the two words that had influenced my life: What If?

"What if we wrote a book together, gearing POS toward the healthcare profession?" I had followed the What-If? Exercise to a whole new level. What if I take the risk to tell this busy and successful author and speaker who I really am, what my goals and challenges are, how I'm trying to use his principles in my practice, and how they have inspired me and could potentially inspire and encourage others? My fear was that I would essentially set out my whole life on paper to a stranger, and he would read two sentences and toss my letter away.

About a week later, my phone rang. Guess who? That's right. It was Scott Gross.

"Greg," he says, "I've got to tell you, I've been doing this business for over 30 years, and I've never received a nine-and-a-half-page letter before. That was awesome. Thank you so much. What really intrigues me is the last paragraph of your letter. It's those two words you wrote, 'What if?'"

We talked over the concept of partnering on a book for a while longer. I remember my new friend ended the conversation by saying, "Greg, I think we're on to something."

Over the next year and a half, we worked on our book. I contributed my experiences in the healthcare field and solutions I had been thinking about for a long time. I was constantly frustrated by how stereotypic the healthcare profession had become.

Think about it. As you walk into your typical medical or dental office, the chairs are lined up around the waiting room, elevator music is playing in the background, and the receptionist has a smoked glass window closed or barely open between you and her, with a sign stuck to the wall saying: *Sign in, sit down, and shut up. I'm too busy to say hello.* On the other side of the window, an inviting sign plastered to the wall says: *Payment is due at the time of service or get the heck out.* That kind of gives you a warm and fuzzy feeling, don't you think? Then they go to all the trouble to prevent you from becoming a thief by welding a 59-cent ballpoint pen to a chain bolted to the wall! Scott saw how it all fit together with the concepts of delivering exceptional service in every aspect of life. Scott had been an EMT in his earlier life, so writing a book for the medical profession hit a soft spot in his heart. Our book came together as *The Service Prescription: Healthcare the Way It was Meant to Be.*

That was my first book and my entrance into the world of publishing. I had gone from business owner and dentist to author. The power of **What If?** Had taken me to a very unexpected place.

✳✳✳

I'm a long way from my sandbox days, but I'm still fascinated by the world of **What Ifs?.**

The longer I play the game and apply it to my own business and personal life, the more I've come to realize that the exercise also fascinates the world's heavy-duty thinkers in corporate leadership, psychology, and even spirituality. It's a deceptively simple idea, but it works. Of course, after you free your mind to ask What If? And allow yourself to dream of possibilities, where do you go from there?

For time after I stepped out of the dental practice that I founded, I just wanted to take a break from it all; I no longer wanted to pursue the *why* of what I did. All my What-If? Dreams were packed away.

Mentally, I had lost most of my willingness and passion to start all over again.

Then, in 2012, my sons Brent and Blake threw down their challenge to me, saying in essence, "Okay, Dad, it's time to go back to doing what you love, and this time the three of us are going to take it to the next level."

Their willingness to tackle a new goal was exactly what I needed to get re-energized. Suddenly, I was ready to get back into the game. When we officially launched ProGrin Dental, we did so based on the principles I had incorporated in my first dental practice. Back in 1983, my commitment to creating *the exceptional experience* for my patients was pretty much built on gut instinct and, of course, Uncle Fred's and Jack Bogart's wisdom.

Three decades later, I was just as committed to creating the Perfect Patient Experience, but I saw that the concept was tied to other patterns I had not necessarily noticed before. Without realizing it, I had employed the very principles that today's motivational experts and corporate strategists recommend. I knew these principles worked; now, I was hungry to know *why*.

DREAMS VS. PLANS

When I discovered Simon Sinek, I saw that other people were asking "why" too. Sinek is a brilliant corporate strategist who is fascinated by successful business leaders and what makes them tick. He got on everyone's radar in 2009 with his first book, *Start With Why: How Great Leaders Inspire Everyone to Take Action*. Sinek is fascinated by the dynamics that make one company succeed and another fail. He examines questions like "What If?" but is most fascinated with the companion question, "Why?"

When I started reading Simon Sinek's books and listening to his talks online, it was like Uncle Fred was standing right next to me. The London-born and educated Sinek was talking about universal concepts of business that my cop-turned-beauty-business-entrepreneur Uncle Fred instinctively knew to be true. These were the concepts that Uncle Fred had passed on to me.

I was eager to learn even more as I built my second company. Like Sinek, I wanted to follow the What Ifs with the Whys. I was fascinated by the qualities that separated an average company from a great one.

The talk by Simon Sinek that revved my thinking into high gear was posted online in 2009 by the TED Conferences. TED is a media organization that posts free talks by the world's greatest thinkers, doers, leaders, scientists, and philosophers. Its slogan, "ideas worth spreading," and its conferences attract the most sought-after speakers in the world. Since it was founded several decades ago, it has expanded beyond its original ideas that explored Technology, Entertainment, and Design (i.e., TED). Now the conferences take on all questions that challenge why human beings do what we do.

Simon Sinek's talk has had 43.5 *million* views online, making it the most popular TED talk ever. Sinek begins by noting a pattern in the history of business and leadership that we all know to be true but is not easily explained.

First, he notes the phenomenon that is Apple. At its core, Apple is just a computer company, right? Why did it become one of the most innovative, most universally recognized, and powerful companies and brands on the planet?

And consider Martin Luther King, Jr. He was an able civil rights leader, but he wasn't the only one to rise to prominence in the 1950s, and he wasn't necessarily one of the movement's greatest orators. So why is he honored today with a national holiday and remembered in every history book?

And what about those two wannabe inventors with the bicycle shop in Dayton, Ohio? Orville and Wilbur Wright were brothers who dropped out of high school, became obsessed with tinkering with machinery, and were often broke. They had a lot of rich and well-heeled competitors trying to develop what they were trying to invent. So why is it that today, the Wright boys are revered as the inventors of man-powered flight?

Here's how Simon Sinek answers those questions: Great leaders and innovators (Steve Jobs, Martin Luther King, the Wright Brothers, etc.) share a unique pattern. Sinek says, "There is a pattern that makes all great leaders think, act, and communicate in the same way, and it's the complete opposite of everyone else."

Sinek's insight is that successful thinking by great leaders is a response to "a naturally occurring pattern grounded in the biology of human decision-making." He calls it "the Golden Circle," and it's an instinctive quality wired in the human brain that intuitively draws people to a person or company.

As best I can explain it, that quality is the hunger to know why something is important and has purpose. The Golden Circle is an instinctive response by human beings that says we want to be connected to others who share our purpose and beliefs. Great organizations and great leaders tap into this pattern—whether deliberately or as a gut instinct—and by doing so, they naturally attract others.

They do it not by just offering a product, technology, or political platform but by infusing "why," they offer it with deeper meaning.

Sinek says that people respond intuitively to the reason behind a business or service; they intuit the why. "The goal is not to sell to people who need what you have; *the goal is to sell to people who believe what you believe.*" In other words, successful businesses and people attract clients, customers, and audiences because they offer a purpose and a meaning that goes deeper than the product, service, or campaign slogan. They give people a reason to believe in something.

So how does that answer the question about Apple, MLK, and the Wright Brothers? Sinek explains it this way: Apple achieved icon status not as "a company that sells computers" but because it communicates the message, *"We are a company that believes in challenging the status quo by thinking differently."* (Oh, and by the way, we build beautiful products that just happen to be computers.)

The Wright brothers? "They were driven by a purpose, a cause, and a belief," Sinek says. Their competitors just wanted to be first and be famous. Orville and Wilbur were driven by something very different: "They believed if they could figure out this flying machine, it would change the course of the world." It did.

Martin Luther King? Sinek points out that Dr. King didn't just say human laws needed to change; he said human laws need to be changed because they are linked to a nobler cause and a higher authority than mere politics or legislative action. Then in one line, Sinek summed up Dr. King's place in history and hit his own argument out of the ballpark: "He gave the 'I Have a Dream' speech. Not the 'I Have a Plan' speech."

Sounds like a "What If?" speech to me!

I was invigorated. It's not that Simon Sinek is the only corporate strategist who ever electrified my thinking—as you'll see, I have many mentors who juice up my ideas—but at that time, Simon Sinek was saying the things I needed to hear.

I have a dream, not a plan.

It had always been my dream to build a business that delivered an exceptional customer/patient experience. I had proven the concept once before. Now my sons had challenged me to do it again. Again, we would call it the "Perfect Patient Experience." Make no mistakes about it; the principles that lit my spark will light yours too!

INTEGRATING LESSONS

What was exciting this time around was to know that I was using concepts that fascinated the best minds in the world of business and the social sciences. Simon Sinek confirmed for me that I was building more than a *plan*—more than just the nuts, bolts, and drills of a dentist's office.

OK, *what if* I consciously and deliberately set out to create a work culture that attracted employees and patients, that gave them an experience they'd never had before? As Sinek says, people have to know *why* you're doing something. He also says, "If they believe in it, they will follow you."

Of course, it begins with the people you hire. Sinek makes the point: "If you hire people just because they can do the job, they'll work for money, but if you hire people who believe what you believe, they will work for you with blood, sweat, and tears." When I read that, I immediately thought of my job interview test with the scrap of trash paper on the floor. I would place a crinkled-up piece of paper on the floor directly in front of where the potential employee would be seated, with a trash can immediately positioned next to the chair. While the individual was patiently waiting for me to walk in to greet them, I wanted to see if they noticed the obvious piece of paper staring at them on the floor, and I was hoping they would instinctively pick up the scrap of paper and toss it into the trash can prior to my walking into the room. I was separating candidates who were just there for the paycheck from the candidates who believed, as I did, in offering the Perfect Patient Experience. If I walked into the room and the paper was still there on the floor, in the back of my mind, the interview was over before it ever began. No questions asked!

I also realized just how important the name of our business was in emphasizing our brand. We were focused on a name that was tied to the entire experience, from the initial phone call to when they left the office. I didn't want it to be just "Greg Ayers, DMD, Family Dentistry." We chose the name ProGrin Dental because we felt it captured the promise of a relaxed, fun, and positive life experience that could change a person's future in wonderful ways. *That* was the business my sons and I wanted to build.

Yes, a pattern was emerging. Every dentist knows what they do and how they do it. The difference with our practice? We know *why* we do it. Question: How about your company?

***

You might think I'm done with the What-If? Game in this chapter, but not quite. First, a little background.

Since 2012, ProGrin Dental has grown steadily and is now in multiple locations in the upstate of South Carolina. People started to notice. To my surprise, we weren't only getting calls from prospective patients; we were getting calls from young dentists just starting out who needed advice. I remember one call from a young doctor who said, "I just bought this practice, and I'm frustrated because it's been in business for 30 years, and I don't know how to take it to the next level. The receptionist has been here forever. She seems to know all the ropes, she knows the patients, and she knows how to do the books. The problem is that she's still mourning her old boss' exit, so she doesn't respect or listen to me, and she doesn't want to change!"

This is a problem I know all too well because we buy existing dental practices, too. That's how we continue to expand to multiple locations. What we're buying isn't just the bricks, mortar, and a patient base; we're buying the entire staff, their expertise, and most importantly, the culture of their company. Folding all these dynamics into our ProGrin culture is our most challenging problem. Change is extremely difficult, especially if a company you are acquiring has been doing it the same way for over 30 years.

You've heard the saying, "If it ain't broke, don't fix it." Sadly, many companies and even individuals live their entire lives with this principle. What I've learned over my career is the exact opposite, "If nothing ever changes, then NOTHING EVER CHANGES!" It's like the definition of insanity, doing the same thing over and over again, day in and day out, and expecting a different result.

At ProGrin Dental, we adopted our own principle, "If it ain't broke, BREAK IT."

**Always continue to improve—
personally, professionally & spiritually.**

As we built our ProGrin business model, we knew we had to start at the beginning, even before the patient walks in the door. And it starts with our culture, the foundational building blocks that make us different. This is true for any successful business. Then it's introducing your culture to the new staff you are acquiring. An experienced staff is good, but unless you consciously build a culture of excellence, too often, experience leads to routine, which leads to boredom, and *that* is the message that gets projected onto the customer or patient. We've all had the frustration of doing business with a company that treats us like a faceless, mindless intrusion on their day. If we can escape and give our business to someone else, we do! Unfortunately, the medical/dental industry is saturated with this culture. Don't get me wrong; there are phenomenal healthcare practices out there that I have the utmost respect for and have learned from. Unfortunately, too many are stuck in the stereotypic rut handed down from one healthcare owner to another over the years.

Instead, we train our team to create an exceptional experience from the moment of our first contact with the public. I like to say that the Perfect Patient Experience always begins with "hello." It could begin with how warmly and inviting the phone is answered to how a new or existing patient is greeted when they walk into your office, or how our employees possibly greet and interact with

36

the checkout lady at the grocery store as they stand there with our ProGrin logo on their scrubs.

What if we answer the phone in such a friendly way that the person on the other end feels like they are the most important person in the world? (Staff: "Well, gosh, it probably will make them happier to make an appointment.")

What if we note in the computer the names of their kids and their spouse so we can ask about their family when they come in? (Staff: "Well, I know I'd like to have somebody ask me about *my* family.") Over time, it became apparent that by pushing people to take that next step with the What-If questions we were building an actual culture of success. My son, Brent, the COO of our company, is especially interested in creating a management style that embodies a mindset and a culture, and that doesn't happen by accident.

Everyone on the team must be trained in our systems—and that means everyone, especially ME!

Over time, what dawned on me was that all the business advice in the world boils down to creating a culture that makes your team, customers, your patients—your audience—feel as if they are participating in something that has purpose and meaning. I realized that was the part of the dream I'd had ever since those sandbox days—to do something special—but I needed the experience to put it all together. Brent calls it "building something that's greater than anything you've ever done."

Challenge on.

CHAPTER THREE

THE 3% DIFFERENCE

We have a sign painted on the wall of one of our conference rooms that sums up the culture of our practice and everything we believe about patient care. Its message is what keeps us centered, focused, and successful. When team members or other doctors and their staff come in for a meeting or tour of our office, they are intrigued by the sign.

The sign says:

At 211 degrees, water is hot.
At 212 degrees, it boils.
With boiling water comes steam, and with steam you can power a train.
One extra degree makes all the difference.

I explain to my guests that the message is about the critical importance of just one extra degree of heat, which is the difference between water flatlining at 211 degrees and water coming to a boil at 212.

That's what I've come to term the *3% difference*. It's also ingrained in everything we deliver at all our ProGrin dental practices—the Perfect Patient Experience. If my audience is interested to know more, I might go on to tell them about Uncle Fred, who unconsciously used the same principle to build a world-class beauty supply business.

What's the message behind the 212-degree sign? **Very small things add up to produce powerful results**. That bit of extra effort could be the difference between being ordinary and *extraordinary*. The closest margin of victory in a NASCAR race is 0.002 seconds! Tell the winning pit crew that small details don't matter when the race car pulls into the pit to refuel or have their tires changed.

The old steam locomotives of the early 1800s were nothing but immobile hunks of steel until their boilers ramped up to 212 degrees. At that point, the water in the boiler tanks started to produce enough steam to allow the trains to take off and reach speeds of over 100 mph—that is if the wooden tracks held up. The difference in degrees Fahrenheit that moved the train from inertia to 100 miles an hour? Just 3% percent. When the steam engine was invented ("perfected" is probably a better word since people have been tinkering with the idea of steam power for over a thousand years), a train was transformed from a lump of machinery dragged by oxen on treadwheels into a bullet that crisscrossed continents. Think of it. Only a 3% difference fueled the Industrial Revolution and changed history.

I like to say, "Great companies just don't only do the big things well; they execute the small things superbly!" It might be something as simple as a receptionist standing up and welcoming you by name instead of just sitting behind a sliding smoke-glass window and not even acknowledging you are there. It offers every person who comes into your office a "comfort menu" from headphones with their favorite artist playing, a headrest pillow, a heated blanket placed over them, scented lip balm, or a steamed scented towel after their dental procedure. Or possibly a coffee bar, bottled water along with freshly baked cookies. It's the 3% difference from being average to exceptional! It's that 30-second follow-up phone call in the evening to check on your patient, client, or customer to make sure their visit to your business went well. Just random, out-of-the-ordinary 3% opportunities to say thank you and express to them that you care.

I can't emphasize this point enough. I struggle to think of a business that doesn't have some sort of human interaction. To unleash the key to your success, all you have to do is to "find your sandbox to sit in." Get quiet and alone and think about the 3% difference you could offer your clients or end users of the products or services you provide. My mentor, T. Scott Gross, taught me well when I read his best-selling book, *POS: Positively Outrageous Service*. When the bar is raised and giving good customer service becomes the norm in your industry, where do you go, what do you do, to differentiate yourself from your competition? You deliver POS!

Don't copy what your competitors are doing. That positions you to forever play catch up! Create your own identity. I remember a copy machine salesman coming into my office to sell us a new state-of-the-art copier. He explained to us all his machine's bells and whistles, but what he said next axed the sale. He said his machine was "just as good as a Xerox!" If that was the case, why don't we just buy the Xerox? We know they are the best in the industry!

41

———

Chart your own course that separates you from the competition.

———

LIGHT BULB HAPPENSTANCE

Have you ever had an aha moment? It happened to me three months after I opened my dental practice. I was attending an out-of-town dental conference. My wife, Sharon, and our three-month-old son came with me. We left after work, and by the time we arrived at our destination city, it was after 11:00 PM. Knowing I was getting up in less than six hours, I took the cheap way out and drove right past an Embassy Suite to a rundown, $19.95 motel down the street. Of course, Sharon put up some resistance, especially with a newborn, but my conscience wouldn't let me spend $250/night for a measly six hours of sleep. You know you're in trouble when the front door to the "no tell motel" is locked, and you have to converse with the check-in lady with a cigarette dangling out of her mouth, through what appeared to be a bulletproof glass window. Trust me; it only got worse from there. Once I found the room, conveniently located at the end of a dark alley, I soon realized the $19.95 I paid was too much. Chunks of the sprayed popcorn ceiling had fallen off and were lying on the bed. The shower door and both hinges were lying on the bathroom floor. I was still hoping Sharon would take one for the team and catch some zzzz's for just a few hours. Needless to say, that wasn't happening. She was fuming and demanded we immediately leave that roach-infested hole!

In the back of my mind, I was thinking that a marital counselor was on the horizon to get me out of this poor decision to save a few bucks. I stormed down the alley and up to the front window and demanded my money back. She said she didn't have a clue how to credit the $19.95 back onto my credit card, but she did have $12.00 cash she could give me. Deal!

Honestly, I don't have a clue what the seminar was about or for that matter who the speaker was. All I knew was that I had a lot of damage control to do to salvage my marriage. I decided to leave the seminar early and made an executive decision to drive two-and-a-half hours to Asheville, North Carolina, and see if there were any vacancies at the five-star Grove Park Inn, located in the beautiful Smokey Mountains. At first, Sharon didn't have a clue where we were heading. She still wasn't talking to me. For all I knew, she probably thought we were heading back home.

When we pulled into the Grove Park Inn parking lot, she perked up with the biggest smile on her face. To be honest with you, in the back of my mind, I was hoping that all the rooms were taken. It's the thought that counts, right? As my luck would have it, a room was available. They informed us that they would take our luggage to our room and invited us to relax and have an enjoyable meal, along with complimentary drinks, on the outside porch with a million-dollar view of the sun setting over the mountains. After eating the delicious meal, we went up to our room. To my surprise, when we walked in, Chad's crib was already set up with the finest linens and blanket, along with a fresh basket of fruit, a small bottle of chilled champagne, and two crystal glasses alongside the bed. To me, they had already hit it out of the park in the short amount of time we had been there.

Then the aha moment hit me… I looked over at the master bed. The covers were pulled down neater than an Army private's bed in the barracks bunk house. But the thing that blew my mind was what was lying directly in the middle of both pillows—a piece of Godiva chocolate! I couldn't get over that. In fact, for the next two weeks, everyone I encountered—from patients to family and friends—I shared with them the "mint on the pillow" story. Then it hit me like a ton of bricks, *That's It! That's the secret to building any successful business!*

———

Look for opportunities to put a mint on the pillow!

———

This applies not just to you but to your entire office staff. Something so small, so inexpensive as a Godiva Chocolate certainly got my attention. The $300+ I spent that night paled in comparison to what I learned from a 50-cent mint on the pillow! I became the best marketing tool the Grove Park Inn ever had, sharing our experience, and topping it off with the "mint on the pillow" story.

Whatever your business, what is it you and your team can do to look for opportunities to do that one small thing that gives your customers or patients their personal aha moment that will have them talking about you and your business for months and years to come? Thirty-six years later, that is still my number-one story to explain how we built and continue to create a very successful business. Heck, as I'm typing this on my computer right now, I still get invigorated about sharing the story with you.

More than anything else, I want this book to inspire you to do yourself a favor and challenge yourself. Just like in a NASCAR race, slow down, pull into the pits, refuel (quality time alone), and imagine what your life, your company, would be like if you…! I'll let you finish that story! That could be your aha moment! Go for it! Don't settle for average, or even second best, but do me this favor: be sure and email me the exciting results in the weeks, months, and years to come as you experience your aha moment!

———

What does a small token have to do with success in business or in life? That 3% difference? Everything.

———

I'm convinced that the concept of the 3% difference is so deceptively simple that most people overlook it, and that's why they remain frustrated and puzzled by the fact they never quite achieved all they hoped for in life. Oh, maybe they feel like they came close, but they carry that image in their minds of their full potential, their ultimate dream of doing something great, and they realize they didn't quite get there. It remains a mirage they missed by only *that much*. They missed filling in that last 3%.

Well, I was determined not to miss it. The kid in the sandbox who wanted to reach for the stars, to do something special, was still kicking inside of me. I couldn't shake it, even after my golf dreams were crushed. As I thought about it, I realized the 3% difference could be applied to every profession and every dream. That got me thinking about the qualities that allow some people to soar in life while other people just live out their allotted span, content to be mediocre or average. That's when it hit me: it's not *what* you do but *how* you do it. In other words, the thing that blocks people from their full achievement and potential is within *you*, so the only thing blocking you is contentment in "just being average."

Being average or blending in with the crowd doesn't set you apart. It takes no effort. It doesn't challenge you! I've always been ticked off and annoyed by let's-just-get-by qualities—anything that's lukewarm, mediocre, and average. It's basically working one day and repeating that same day over and over again for the next 40 years. Is that what you want from this short life you're blessed to have? Maybe it's because I worked so hard to overcome every challenge that could possibly entrap *me* in those qualities. As I've said to my kids, staff, and friends, "Being average is like eating wet bread or kissing your sister." It's like going to a fast-food joint and ordering a cheeseburger with fries. You don't go home, call all your friends, and say, "I just had the most unbelievable cheeseburger in my whole life." No, a fast-food cheeseburger is a fast-food cheeseburger. It's nothing to talk about. Maybe I should rephrase that and say if a cheeseburger/fries does inspire you, then we need to have a more serious and in-depth conversation.

My point is, to take your business beyond wet bread or fast-food cheeseburgers, you must aspire to be above average. How? The key is, we all have to look for opportunities to *put the mint on the pillow.* That's any kind of genuine, unexpected, extra gesture that makes people feel valued and special. It doesn't matter if the business is the hospitality industry, financial services, dentistry, or a bagel shop; there are always opportunities to create a beautiful moment for customers. And, yes, you can create that experience even in the cheeseburger industry. I'm proof that it's never forgotten when you take the time to do that.

That's why in my business I challenge every individual on my team, whether they are a hygienist or dental assistant, a front office administrator, or one of my fellow dentists: "What are you doing to put mint on the pillow?" How are you making that experience extra special for the patient? If you happen to be in another profession, sit down and make your own list! You'll be glad you did!

THE EXTRA MILE

In our company, we consider this step of training—finding ways to deliver the Perfect Patient Experience— which is so important that my son Brent and I, along with our entire management team, have assembled a training team and program to make sure every new person who joins us understands this important concept. It is the culture of who we are at ProGrin Dental or iGrin Children's Dentistry. It begins, of course, with the basic "meet and greet" qualities of our prospective dentists, hygienists, and staff. Doesn't everything begin with "hello?" Do they know how to project confidence in their voice and manner? Do they know how to engage in an easy conversation, and do they have the compassion to ask about the patient's family? Do they make eye contact, have a firm handshake, and generally present friendly, accessible professionalism?

You may think these are basic, common-sense qualities that every business would expect from their employees, and of course they are.

Then there are the qualities that define the culture of a business. There is a reason why Chick-fil-A is the gold standard in the fast-food industry. Their employees are always warm and smiling. When they hand you your order, and you respond with "thank you," their response back to you is never "You're welcome" but rather "My pleasure." That is not by accident. That is a learned culture derived from implementing customer-centered systems and in-depth training programs. Likewise, the mint on the pillow just didn't happen by accident at the Grove Park Inn. It was a part of their culture that happens every time and every night when they pull the sheets back. In my profession, these same qualities are critical, but they are tailored to our particular culture. Let me put it this way: Resort hotels rank pretty high on the "fun" scale, while going to the dentist doesn't rank on the "top ten" list of things to do and places to go. What a great opportunity! Patients hate going to the dentist because that is what they've always done—go to the dentist! They've never had the pleasure of being on the receiving end of the PPE!

The success of our company has more to do with the exceptional service and care patients receive than the product—i.e., dental procedures.

Don't get me wrong. We pride ourselves in providing great dental services and care, but what drives our customers/patients back is the experience they have while in our office. From the moment they pull into our parking lot to when they leave, they are playing in our sandbox now, and each member of our team has a role to play in delivering the Perfect Patient Experience. Not just some of them or when they feel like it, but all of them, all the time. And, as the boss, I have to walk the talk at an even higher level than I expect my team to do. Those who don't buy into our culture stick out like a sore thumb. We attempt to retrain, but if their behavior doesn't change, as I like to say, "We don't fire them…they fire themselves."

Then add on that magical 3% that occurs after the patient leaves; the patient experience kicks up to an even higher level than they have ever experienced before! You have a patient/customer for life who has now turned into the marketing arm of your company, referring all their family, friends, and co-workers to you! I call it the Eighth Wonder of the World!

PERFECTION!

To sum it all up, to build a dynamic and thriving company, delivering the perfect experience is paramount! Whether you aim for the Perfect Patient Experience (PPE) or the Perfect Customer Experience (PCE), this approach makes missionaries out of your customers/patients! I thought it was so important that I entitled it, the **Circle of Influence (COI)**.

You see, everyone has people that they communicate with daily, weekly, or monthly. Their COI may include a husband or wife, girlfriend or boyfriend, mother, father, brothers, sisters, aunts, uncles, neighbors, co-workers, little league baseball and soccer families, church members…the list goes on. These are the folks your customers communicate with on a regular basis. You start with one customer and give them the best, over-the-top experience they've have ever had. When they leave, I assure you they will be on their cell phone before they ever leave your parking lot calling someone on their COI. I will bet my last dollar that this recipient of the PCE or PPE will become a raving fan of your business. The result or return on investment (ROI) on delivering the PCE/PPE is the number of new customers that almost immediately begin calling your office or place of business wanting to make an appointment for themselves and, quite often, their entire family.

CIRCLE OF INFLUENCE

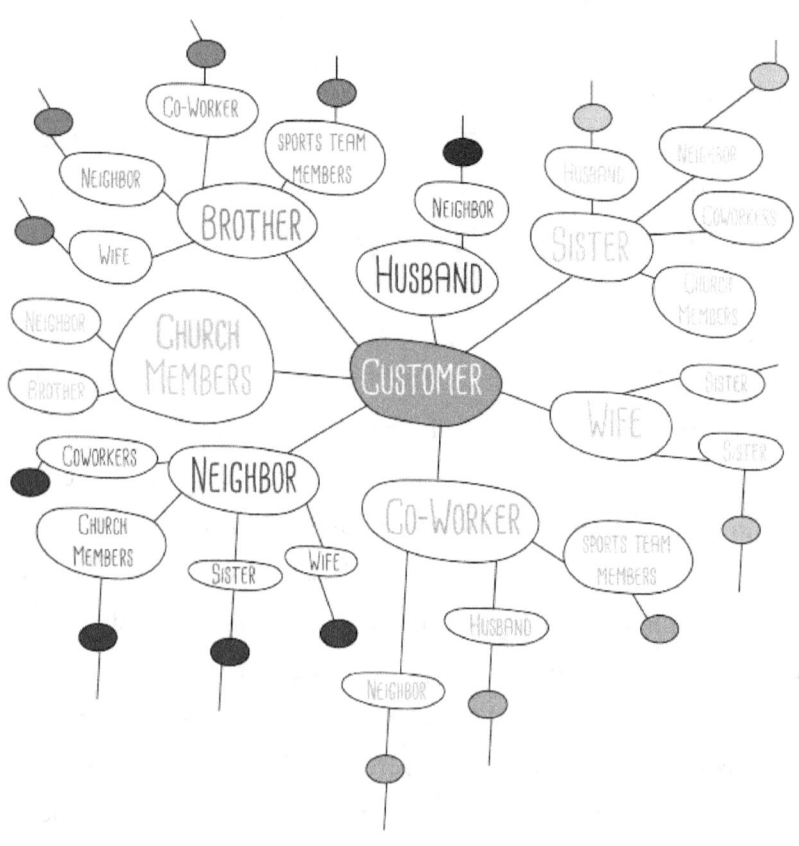

When the new patient who was referred arrives for their first appointment, guess what? The PPE/PCE game starts all over again because this new customer/patient has a different set of friends on their COI than the person who referred them. That's how I've built my dental company, and Uncle Fred built his highly successful beauty-supply company over the years. One customer or patient "infected" with the PCE/PPE tells their friends/family in their own COI. This experience repeated over and over again. It's not rocket science!

In today's world, everyone's COI is exponentially bigger than it used to be, thanks to Google and social media platforms. The COI 1.0, which I've been talking about over the past 15 years, consisted of building direct, one-on-one relationships with your customers/patients.

If the customer received a great experience, they would have to verbally tell their family and friends about it. Word-of-mouth referrals were king. That's not to discount the value of word-of-mouth referrals in today's world; they are still vital and important to your business' success. It's just that in the world we live in today, customers can literally spread good or bad news about your business to the entire world in a matter of seconds via Google, Yelp, Facebook, etc. reviews. Their COI now spans far beyond people they know personally.

Think about it. If you're in the mood to try out a new restaurant, what's the first thing you typically do? Call your neighbor to see if they've eaten there? Probably not. Most likely, you are going to Google the name of the restaurant and check out their online reviews. If the restaurant has an overall rating of 2 stars, I doubt you'll waste your time going there. Alternatively, if they have 1000+ 5-star reviews, you've got no choice but to taste it for yourself. In today's world, the opinions of complete strangers heavily influence our buying decisions. So, unlike 15 years ago, when the average person's COI may have been 100 people, today their COI consists of millions of people. The COI 2.0 is an unbelievable opportunity for business growth so long as you're providing a great product/service and a world-class customer experience. Conversely, the COI 2.0 can be how your business fails if you aren't exceeding your customers' expectations. If the COI 1.0 was the entire Earth, COI 2.0 is the entire Universe.

It's vastly larger and moves at the speed of light. You can no longer afford to let upset customers leave unsatisfied because of the speed at which they can inform an audience of millions. Think about it, in less time than it takes for an unsatisfied customer to pull out of your parking lot, they could have already posted on their Facebook about how much you suck, left you 1-star reviews on all the major review boards, and still have time to pick up their cell phone and tell their friend about their sub-par experience. If you have the slightest inkling that a customer isn't 100 percent satisfied, don't wait for them to leave, hoping they aren't upset.

Instead, politely ask them in private about their experience and just listen to them and do whatever it takes to make things right. I can assure you letting them leave without addressing it is your most costly option. You also have to train your team on how to identify these situations and empower them to do whatever it takes to make it right. Some of our most loyal patients didn't start off by having the most positive experience, but we acknowledged to them that we dropped the ball and bent over backward to make it right. And now we have a patient for life!

———

The Perfect Patient/Customer Experience encourages your customers to become missionaries for your business.

———

I like to say the penalty of delivering a product this appealing is the demand of customers and patients eagerly wanting to come to see you, a demand that often becomes challenging. I like to say you can only get so many sardines in a can, no matter how good they are. That's when you have to think outside the box and decide whether you might need to hire more employees, another doctor or staff member, or even expand into another location. Protecting your brand is so critical when you make the move to expand. You have to build a solid management team who can recruit, train and set the train in motion to duplicate what made you so successful in the beginning.

***

People who feel comfortable, valued, and well-treated become our best ambassadors. Of course, the opposite is also true, especially in this age of social media where each person's opinion becomes instantly powerful. We all do it. Have you noticed that when we find a product or service we love or hate, most of us suddenly turn into ace consumer advocates or roving critics? We go out in the world on all these daily adventures to buy tires, a new car, or to try out a new gym. Then when we get back, we have war stories we want to share with others.

The type of review I'm aiming for sounds like this: "I know you have a toothache that comes and goes. You've got to try my dentist.

He always finds the problem and fixes it, and besides that, he and the staff are just amazing to be around. I always leave there feeling good! The doctor even called that evening to check on me."

That kind of review sums up our dentistry culture: Fix the problem (number one) and make patients feel at ease while we do it. In the age of social media, a great or terrible experience at your business can go viral within minutes of your customer leaving.

Keeping those reviews positive always starts with the quality of the people you hire. It doesn't matter if it's your auto mechanic, the manager at your neighborhood grocery store, or your financial advisor. If the auto mechanic misplaces your keys for a day, or the grocery store leaves spilled boxes in the aisles, or the receptionist at the financial firm always looks glum when you walk in—these small things make customers uneasy. They communicate that something may be "off " about the business itself.

Put it the opposite way: the sharp mechanic who has your keys always ready and washes your windows before you leave; the shiny floors at the grocery and the produce section are neat and fully stocked, and the happy receptionist who greets you by name—these small things add up to be the 3% difference that drives customer confidence and loyalty. The lesson is that **great companies don't just do the big things well; they execute the small details superbly.**

***

We've all heard the expression, "You never get a second chance to make a first impression."

———

That's why I've never understood businesses that don't invest well in the person who greets people at the front desk. They are the gatekeeper to your business.

———

These gatekeepers answer incoming calls, greet patients like invited guests into your home, and schedule and check out customers and/or patients. They set the tone for the entire customer experience. We have an important title for these valuable team members; they are the "Director of First Impressions." That type of mindset is really a software issue between your brain and your heart. I think it is very difficult, if not just plain impossible, to train someone to have a great personality. It's inherently embedded in their DNA. I could be wrong on this, but my 35+ years of experience tell me otherwise.

One of my favorite dental mentors, Linda Miles, had a saying that I have never forgotten. "Your attitude determines your altitude." I can't say it any better. People with infectious positive attitudes always see the glass as half full versus half empty. People with great attitudes pump you up and breathe new life into you versus those negative-minded people who suck the air right out of you and possibly your entire organization. Like a virus, they can slowly grow, and before you know it, half of your team is infected, and now you have a major pandemic on your hands. Remember to hire slow and fire fast!

***

Understanding how to deliver that extra 3% sometimes makes for a memorable experience.

One morning back in the early 1990s, Sandy, my office manager, waved me down to say there was a call I should take. It was from one of my patients, Linda, who happened to be the human resources executive with one of the world's best-known tire manufacturing companies. This company built its U.S. corporate headquarters one block from my office. Lucky for me! Many of my patients were employees there. This company was merging with another internationally known tire company, and executives from around the world were meeting in the Greenville corporate office to discuss the upcoming merger.

When I answered the call, Linda said, "Dr. Ayers, we're in a big bind. The chairman of the board for company X just called me. He just landed in Atlanta and has an important board meeting this afternoon at 1:30. The problem is, the crown on his front tooth just broke off at the gum line! He's scheduled to make the lead presentation to the officers and directors of the merging companies, and he's missing his front tooth! Is there anything you can do?"

I didn't miss a beat; even though, at that instant, I didn't know quite how we were going to make it work. "As soon as he lands, bring him right over. We'll be waiting for him."

I gathered my staff and told them that our lunch plans were out the window. I've always told my staff and associate doctors that our #1 practice builder is an emergency patient in crisis.

"Everyone, let's pull together and give Mr. X the best dental experience of his life!"

Like a well-rehearsed pit stop, everyone in the office had a role to play. The moment Mr. X stepped foot in the office, it was game on! We welcomed him to our practice and extended to him the PPE we take pride in delivering. It didn't matter that we were working through our lunch hour. To him, he felt as if he was the most important person on the planet, and he just happened to be in a dental office, of all places! Within an hour, we took an x-ray, placed a post and buildup inside his front tooth, and re-cemented his crown back on. We handed him the mirror and exclaimed, "Just like new!" You could sense his sigh of relief after we restored his smile. He couldn't find the words to express his gratitude. He got to his meeting with his confident smile restored with fifteen minutes to spare.

Now, you're going to think that's the 3% difference, but it's only part of it. The best is yet to come! As this executive was being escorted by our caring staff to our front desk, he was thanking us from the bottom of his heart, completely relieved and blown away that we could help him so quickly. As he held out his credit card to pay the bill, our administrative staff eagerly awaited him. They knew exactly what to do and say because we had rehearsed the scenario in advance. As he held out his credit card, my staff said, "Mr. X, we are honored to be able to assist you with your dental emergency. There is no charge for today's visit. We're so glad Linda, your human resource executive, called us. Your company is highly respected in our town and is the largest and most loyal part of our dental family. We are just happy to be able to give something back in return."

The look on his face was priceless. We shook hands, and as we escorted him out, I could tell by the set of his shoulders and his jaunty step that he was experiencing the euphoria of a guy who had just seen his day flip from disaster to delight in one hour.

Here's the capper to the story. An hour later, I get a call from Linda, the executive who set up the whole encounter. "Dr. Ayers, I've just got to tell you something. For probably 20 minutes, Mr. X was raving to everybody in the board room about the most memorable positive experience in customer service he had ever experienced. The moment he sat down in your chair, he was convinced you and your team were going to come to his rescue and do it fast. Now he's telling everybody, 'If you need a great dentist in the Greenville area, go see Dr. Greg Ayers.' You couldn't have asked for a better endorsement or a better advertisement for your practice if you had hired the top advertising firm in the country!"

I immediately shared with our team the kind words from Linda about the Perfect Patient Experience we just delivered. "You guys were superb—the way you adjusted to this crisis, gave up your lunch hour, and stayed late. We far exceeded our patient's expectations, but just wait and see what happens next." You see, I knew what was coming because we had delivered this type of emergency service many times throughout my dental career.

Sure enough, the following week, the phones began to ring off the hook with employees from this company wanting to schedule appointments for themselves and their families.

That's the magic that separates great companies from average companies. In this case, notice how the 3% difference unfolded in three parts:

- First, we didn't consider the obstacles to tackling the executive's crisis or consider it an inconvenience for working through lunch; we said yes and were confident we could work out whatever details that came up to restore his smile.

- Second, we were so team-oriented that everyone pulled together without complaint. There were no sighs over a lost lunch or a long evening ahead. Every person on the staff grabbed their oars and began to pull.

- Finally, none of it would have happened without Sandy, our office manager. From the beginning, she started the train roaring down the tracks by taking the call from our patient, Linda. Unfortunately, most offices would have said, "We're sorry, but we are at lunch from 1:00-2:00. We could see Mr. X tomorrow afternoon at 3:45." Basically, the receptionist is politely saying, "Sorry for your dental emergency, but you're not going to screw up our lunch hour."

Sandy understood our practice's culture of delivering the Perfect Patient Experience, so she went above and beyond being an average manager who is only trained to be pleasant and efficient and not rock the boat. Instead, Sandy *lived* the 3% difference. She knew how to add that extra one degree and to make the water boil and, yes, put the mint on the pillow!

IS A HAMBURGER THE SAME AS A HAMBURGER?

One of my most effective teaching moments about the 3% difference began the day I called a meeting with my office staff, which at that time, was about sixteen people, and I asked them out to lunch.

"This lunch is on me," I said. "I'm taking you out to lunch every Wednesday for the next three weeks. After lunch, we're gonna talk about some things you all observed. Okay?"

The general feedback was, "That's cool. I'm up for a free lunch." On the first day, I gave them final instructions. "Before we go, let's understand that the guy who controls the gold or has the money gets to make the rules. That's me."

They looked at me like, "Sure, we get it. Can we get going? We're hungry!" I continued, "So when you go, you *must* order either beef, chicken, or fish. Whatever you pick today, you must order that same protein every time for the next three weeks."

Now I saw little smiles appearing here and there, and the group was looking at me like, "What the heck is this guy talking about?" But I knew that *they* knew something was up because they know me.

For that first lunch, I took them to a cheap little hamburger joint called The Clock. The name is pretty clever because I'm guessing it refers to the fact the customers are on the clock and need fast food fast. When we got there, we were hustled into a long line like cattle moving through a gate, and when we got to the counter, the order-taker—a guy with crazed eyes who looked like he was ready to jump off a ledge—was yelling into a little microphone, *"One cheeseburger, lettuce, tomato, hold the onions, extra pickles, ketchup, mayonnaise, order of fries, small tea!"*

Each of us blurted out our choice of protein (chicken, beef, or fish), and the order whizzed through the air to the kitchen. In less than 60 seconds, out came lunch, stapled together with wax paper. We got back to the office, and one by one, I asked each person to tell me about their experience having lunch that day at The Clock.

"Okay, Sandy, what did you get, and what was your experience like?"

"Well, I got a cheeseburger, fries, and a tea. It tasted OK." "Sandy, elaborate more about the entire experience."

"After they took my order and handed me my food on a plastic tray, my cheeseburger and fries were wrapped in cellophane and stapled together; ketchup was in those plastic packs that you have to rip open with your teeth. A plastic fork was wrapped with a thin cheap napkin, tea was in a paper cup, and when you needed a refill, you had to march to the front and wait in line again."

One by one, each person shared their lunch story experience eating beef, chicken, or fish, and all I said in response was, "OK, guys, thanks for the feedback. Next Wednesday, we're going to have lunch again."

The following week, I took them to Ryan's Family Steakhouse. It's one of those places where families love to take their children because kids eat free! Customers walk through a cattle line back and forth until they grab their tray, stainless-steel silverware, and napkin and order their beef, chicken, or fish at the cash register. Afterward, I took the staff through the same drill. "Tell me about your experience."

They talked about how the burgers/chicken/fish came on a plastic plate, the cashier was cordial, the silverware was metal, not plastic, the tea now came in a plastic cup, and somebody actually came by the table to refill their drinks. The ketchup came in a bottle, not plastic packs. Ryan's even had their rendition of the 3% experience by providing free ice cream and freshly baked cookies at the refreshment bar. Overall, a step up from The Clock.

The third week arrived. This time, I took them to Thornblade, a very prestigious country club located practically next door to our office. I had arranged to have the maître d' greet us near the door in his tuxedo and escort us to the president's board room, where a line of waiters was standing with white linen draped over their arms.

We sat at a huge mahogany inlaid table, dressed in the finest china, gleaming silverware, and the finest goblet glasses. The fine linen napkins were carefully placed on our laps. The menu was presented with our office logo on the top and the chef's recommendations of beef, chicken, or fish. The wait staff gracefully replaced a half-filled tea glass with a fresh glass. The meals were delivered on pristine china. It was like poetry in motion, watching everyone have an experience eating a delicious meal.

As we were leaving, the talk from the team was something like, "That was the finest, most amazing meal I've ever had."

When we returned to the office, the excitement from the team was contagious. Everyone was eager to express their memorable experience. I told them I'd been waiting for this moment for three weeks. I informed them that the hamburger meal I bought at The Clock cost me $7.75. The same meal at Thornblade was $19.50. My question to each of them was this: "Is a hamburger the same as a hamburger? After all, they both come from a cow, right? If you were charged $19.50 for your burger at The Clock, what would your reaction be? At the same time, if you paid $19.50 at Thornblade and received The Clock service, how would you feel?" I continued speaking as I pulled a red plastic bowl out of a sack from under the table. "If you picked up your hamburger steak from your china plate at Thornblade and placed it in this red plastic bowl, and then placed the bowl on the floor, what do you have?" At that point, I pulled out an extra Thornblade hamburger and set it in the dish. As I moved the dish to the floor, I rotated the bowl to reveal "Rover" printed on its side.

The group looked at me wide-eyed as if I had suddenly gone crazy. I shouted, "You have dog food!"

***

So, let me ask you, is Thornblade in the business of selling hamburgers? Absolutely not! They are in the business of selling you an experience in fine dining that spurs you to return with family and friends. Plain and simple.

When a person calls our office inquiring about how much it costs to get their teeth cleaned, my question to our staff is, "Are we really in the teeth cleaning business? You can go to any office in town to have that procedure done, or for that matter, you can go to Greenville Technical College and have them cleaned at a fraction of the cost. The product we are delivering is an experience like no other in dentistry. That's the magic sauce. It's the PPE!" The good news is that everything I have said here can be adopted in any business you are in. Remember, the product you should be selling may not be the product being shipped out the door.

———

What would a 3% difference look like in your business?

———

CHAPTER FOUR

MENTORS: KEEPER OF THE GOALS

One of the most inspirational figures in my life was once a dejected alcoholic slumped over on a bar stool. In his earlier life, he had been flying military missions in World War II, and after the war, he found a job as an insurance salesman. Then he lost his way in life and ended up homeless, sleeping on a park bench. My future mentor despised himself for it. Cold and hungry, he peered through the glass of a pawn shop, and despairing of his situation, he saw the solution: a cheap revolver hanging on the wall.

For some miraculous reason, he didn't purchase that gun. I want to believe God intervened in his life that night and convinced him that there was a better way and that he still had dreams and ambitions to pursue. Instead, he went on to become one of the world's most important motivational speakers and authors, and that is how he is remembered.

Og Mandino didn't become a success because he put the gun down and got a job. He became a success because he was able to use his experiences in life to inspire other people to figure out ways to turn the corner on whatever was holding them back from fulfilling their dreams. His breakthrough book, *The Greatest Salesman in the World,* was inspired by the premise that bad habits are the shackles that imprison people and keep them from moving forward. He called on people to recognize life as a miracle and to live with confidence. All his motivational books inspire me to this day.

After Uncle Fred, I have to say Og Mandino was the second figure who inspired me to see life, both personal and professional, from a different perspective. Since finding Mandino's books, I have found many other mentors—I'm always hungry for what I can learn from others—but Mandino's message about keeping daily goals, crushing bad habits, and staying confident and positive was a key influencer for me.

———

**You know where you want to go.
Mentors are the guides who get you there.**

———

Helping young men or women define their goals is the number one job of a mentor. Mentors act as guides and navigators. If a mentor does his or her job right, they sometimes even become heroes.

Once you have asked the *Why,* the *How,* and the *What Ifs,* you have to be smart about defining your goals. I like to think in these terms:

- BE SPECIFIC – Define exactly what your goals are. Write them down. Think them through.
- MAKE SURE THEY ARE MEASURABLE – If you set a goal, you want to make sure you can monitor your progress along the way. Devise some means of measuring your progress.

- MAKE SURE IT IS ACHIEVABLE – Is your goal in sync with your abilities? Not every goal is, so take the time to be honest with yourself.
- BE REALISTIC – Ask yourself whether you are biting off more than you can chew. Along the way, don't short-sell yourself.
- MAKE SURE IT IS TIME-BOUND AND CLEAR – The
- question here is: Can you accomplish your goal in a defined and definite period of time? Having a set schedule – yes, one that can be adjusted – is a smart idea. It keeps you focused and on task.

Once you've been *smart about defining your goals,* the next step is to ignite the spark. In other words, you need some form of energy if you want to take your dream from a beautiful creative gas swirling around in your mind to a concrete plan that you can devise in your head.

BE UNCONVENTIONAL

When I opened my first business in 1983, my only patients were my parents and in-laws. Truthfully, I had very little idea about how to build my patient base, except that something inside of me was convinced I could accomplish something special with my life; I just had to figure out how to get there.

At that point, I didn't know what I didn't know. One truth stood out: I didn't want to spend my life in mediocrity, in an ordinary stereotypic dental practice, working 8-5, 4 ½ days per week. Too often, the profession you are in is very conventional and stereotypic. I have been in countless dental offices, and too often, they are designed the same way. I like to say they look, smell, sound, and feel the same way. If you've been in the typical dentist's office, you know what I mean.

Lucky for me, my first mentor was world-class and as close as our family tree—my mother-in-law's brother, Uncle Fred, who built one of the most successful beauty supply companies in America. His secret sauce was composed of simple but powerful ingredients that he mixed to perfection every day to give his customers a product called *service excellence.*

I resolved to do what Uncle Fred did, but to apply it to dentistry. The amazing thing about delivering service excellence is that it applies to every business. Our ingredients were the same. Assemble a well-trained staff and teach them to implement your vision: *to treat each customer as if you started your business just for them.*

Stay Alert –
Your Next Mentor May Be Walking in the Door Right Now!

A week after graduating from dental school, I was unpacking boxes at my first office when, out of the blue, an insurance salesman named Jack Coggins walked in and introduced himself. (It turns out that Jack would be the man to introduce me to Og Mandino, so you can imagine how glad I was that he walked into my office that day).

What impressed me most about Jack was that he was more interested in helping me get set up, unloading boxes, and taking out empty boxes to the dumpster than trying to sell me life and disability insurance. I had just met a new mentor and friend who would have a major impact on me.

Jack, like myself, was just getting started in his career. What instantly struck me about Jack was that he was more interested in my success than his own. That day, he gave me a book as a kind of "welcome to the neighborhood" present. "I promise you, this book will change your life and the way you do business," he said.

The book was a thin paperback published about fifteen years earlier (in 1968) and written by—yes, you guessed it—Og Mandino. That night, I opened it because I was curious and skeptical about a book that could be so powerful. Well, I didn't put it down until I reached the end at 2:00 a.m.

"Wow," I thought, "this is an Uncle Fred book." Everything Uncle Fred taught me was wrapped up in this book.

Shortly after that, Uncle Fred came to town for a visit, and I couldn't wait to fill him in on the way his ideas and stories had positively impacted my new dental practice. Also, I couldn't wait to share with him the book by my new mentor, Og Mandino. When he stopped by to visit, I said, "Uncle Fred, I've just read this phenomenal book. The guy sounds just like you. Have you ever heard of an author by the name of Og Mandino?"

Uncle Fred was a short, wiry guy weighing maybe 145 pounds, a sparkplug of energy. He staggered back a little, pretending to be surprised, and a big grin bloomed on his face. "Og? Og is my mentor! He's my hero!" I was confused and a little deflated because I thought I could finally tell Uncle Fred something he didn't already know. It turned out that for years Uncle Fred had been buying copies of *The Greatest Salesman in the World*—buying them by the case! He tied each book with a red ribbon and handed it out to every new employee as his gift, saying, "Welcome to the company! The lessons in this book are our company credo. Read and learn."

Og Mandino went on to write many books, and even though he died in 1996 at the age of 72, his legacy continues.

Og is famous for creating the Ten Scrolls, starting with: "Today I begin a new life." Each one is a resolution to make for *today*. They can be summarized like this:

———

Greet each new day with love, persist until you succeed, recognize your existence is a miracle, acknowledge that each day is a gift that may not be repeated, resolve to master your emotions, laugh at the world, multiply your value, act decisively in the present, and pray for guidance.
-Adapted from The Greatest Salesman in the World by Og Mandino (1968)

———

Once he began following these principles himself, Og Mandino became free.

He changed himself, and then he changed Uncle Fred, and eventually, he changed me.

JACK BOGART

A much-repeated Chinese proverb says, "A journey of a thousand miles begins with a single step." This certainly applies to the journey of building a business from scratch, especially a 1,100 square-foot house turned into a dental office, opposite a cow pasture on a two-lane country road, located five miles from nowhere.

Even after I recognized the importance of service excellence, my goal was out on the horizon somewhere because I still had to build my business. I remembered how I hung onto the words of that billboard along the highway, "There is No Heavier Burden than a Great Opportunity." You can say that again!

I knew I needed a mentor to show me how to take those small steps that would lift the burden and reach my dream. I was blessed to find that mentor among one of my very first patients.

He was a remarkable, one-of-a-kind guy named Jack Bogart.

I think Jack and I first connected because he was impressed by the reception he received when he walked in. I already had the PPE in mind, and Jack, like my other patients, was greeted like family. We treated him like we built the entire dental practice just for him and his beautiful wife, Diane. That was our mindset—to appreciate every patient. I like to say to our patients, "We work for you; you don't work for us." The same applies to you if you want to build a dynamic business founded on service excellence. Jack had that same passion for excellence. The difference was he spread it out over an amazingly wide span of professions. At the early age of 17, he became an artist for Walt Disney, working on the classic Disney film, *Snow White and the Seven Dwarfs*. He later left the comfortable world of fantasy to become a fighter pilot in World War II, was shot down during the Ploesti raids over Romania and was rescued in the Mediterranean Sea. He later served in the Korean War, earning the Distinguished Flying Cross and Purple Heart and other high military decorations.

He was a bank president and a marketing and training consultant for some of the country's most influential corporations. Jack's awesome breadth of achievements continued in high gear right up until his death in 2004 at the age of 83. Jack died too soon, not just because he was so deeply mourned by his beautiful family, his wife Diane, and all of us who knew him—though that was certainly true. Jack *literally* died too soon because, at the time, he was still writing articles and working on submitting a patent for a medical device! Jack taught me that at any age, you have something to contribute. Besides the fact I was proud to have such a vigorous and inventive guy as my friend and mentor, I've highlighted his life because I want to point out that with all his achievements, Jack was glad to step into the role of guide and mentor early on in my business.

Maybe if I had read his impressive resume before meeting him in the dental chair, I would have been too intimidated to ask for his help. But Jack was naturally curious, and as he questioned me about my philosophy of business, we naturally clicked. He was intrigued with my profession, which was far outside the realm of a former fighter pilot-banker-businessman-civic leader. That made him even more eager to help.

—————

Never be intimidated to ask someone to be your mentor. The busiest and most successful people are the most honored to help.

—————

Working with Jack was a never-ending creative process. As Jack liked to say, "Building a dynamic business is a journey, not a destination."

I'll never forget Jack asking me what my goal was *after* I had created the PPE. "We know you'll get there," he said, "so what happens after that?"

It's scary when someone challenges you to think about what comes "after that." That's what Jack Bogart forced me to do. A good mentor challenges the status quo and makes things a little uncomfortable.

———

A good mentor forces you to look around the next corner, even before you think you're ready.

———

For quite a while, an idea was building in me. I believed so strongly in my model of delivering service excellence and creating the PPE, and it was working! What better way to cap this successful idea and to expand the patient experience than to duplicate it in multiple locations? It was a natural progression, and I knew it. But at the time, I had only one dental associate working for me and one location. What stymied me was how to get there from here.

I knew the PPE was exploding the popularity of the practice, but what I didn't see yet was how to manage the expanding mushroom cloud of patients and duplicate it in other locations. Jack Bogart was the person who got me to first, articulate the dream, and, next, showed me how to scale it to fit my business. Jack knew how to develop a business plan and an action plan that would allow me to expand to multiple locations.

It was as if I had discovered the spark that ignited the fuse, which launched the rocket. I just didn't know where to aim it.

**You build the launch pad and ignite the dream.
Mentors are your flight control.**

Jack saw the path forward right away. He was very methodical about it. He saw it in terms of taking the satisfaction of one patient and making that one experience explode into many hundreds of satisfied patients, or, as we discussed earlier, the COI.

When you give your customer/patient an experience like they've never had before, I can assure you that they will become the best marketer and raving fan your business has ever had. If one patient or customer is blown away by the exceptional, unexpected service they receive at your business or their dental office, they can't help but tell other people in their COI. Soon the phones begin to ring, and customers/patients begin walking in the door wanting to experience the same thing as their friend.

This concept is so simple yet so important to grasp. If you have a "widget" to sell and your livelihood depends on it, and three other competitors in your town sell the same one, you better lock yourself in the room and figure out the secret sauce that sets yourself and your company apart from the competition.

Thanks to Jack, we just didn't sit down and wait for the phones to ring; we made sure it was very intentional. Jack, with his great organizational skills, methodically drew up concrete ideas to draw more and more people into our dental family. When a prospective patient called, we would immediately send out a handwritten welcome letter on our finest stationery. If they were referred by somebody, they, in turn, received a handwritten thank you referral letter, too. We implemented a system to track those missionaries in our practice who referred their family and friends on their COI to us. We didn't want to bore them by sending them the same thank you referral letter every time. Each one was a little more personal. After so many referrals, we stepped up the game and would send them Starbucks gift cards, flowers, edible arrangements to their place of business, and restaurant gift certificates. Honestly, the list goes on how we acknowledge our referring VIPs to our practice.

I've heard rumblings about how some of my colleagues would say something like, "I can't see how they can afford to send a husband and wife out to the finest restaurant in town. My response is, how can I afford not to? Look at it like this: if I invested a hundred dollars and sent a couple out to dinner for referring three families to our practice over the past two months, wouldn't you think that was a great return on your investment? What is the value of three families over the life of your career? It could well be over $50,000-$100,000! Now, throw in all the referrals they generate, and you get the picture! Now you're in a unique position where you can give back to the community and those less fortunate.

I learned years ago that if you reward or recognize good behavior, you will continue to receive good behavior. Conversely, if you reward poor performance, you'll continue to get poor performance. For example, if an employee is giving you poor or subpar work performance and you decide to give them a raise hoping their attitude will improve in their job performance, odds are they won't. They might improve for a short time, but sooner than later, they will be right back to doing what they've always done. Remember, when you reward results from great performers, you will continue to get rewarded with great results. However, if you reward employees who aren't "cutting the mustard," unfortunately, you'll probably be frustrated with poor results from them.

This principle applies to customers/patients as well. When you acknowledge and reward patients who refer their family and friends to you, I assure you that they will open the floodgates to your company by sending their neighbors, family, and friends to you. How do I know? I've witnessed it firsthand over the past 35 years.

If you do it right, your customers become the best marketing arm of your company!

Several years ago, I was attending a class reunion, and a number of my classmates were sitting around discussing marketing ideas that we all were doing to grow our practices. I shared with them that we gave every new patient at their initial exam a nice ceramic coffee mug with our office logo imprinted on it. I said we invested around $1000 on coffee mugs last year. One of my classmates blurted out, "That's the stupidest idea I've ever heard!" Fast forward 20 years. The return on our investment doing something so simple as giving our new patients coffee mugs is amazing. I can't tell you how many patients were referred to us because they saw our office mug on a co-worker's desk.

Just one referral more than pays for the entire investment for the year on the mugs! So, I'm glad I didn't cave into his advice!

FINDING YOUR MENTOR

I wish I could say that I was a smart guy, but instead, I like to think I just hung around a lot of smart people. Don't isolate yourself. Reach out in every possible way to make a new connection, to seek out your next mentor. The Action Plan at the end of this chapter will give you a few idea jolts to get that started.

_____

Mentors turn up when least expected, so be on the lookout! Know what you need, what you lack, and don't be afraid to ask.

_____

Never miss an opportunity to ask. Successful people always have a reserve of energy and curiosity for the world around them. In fact, I know it's true for me. We want to pass on what we know. When I sign my books for people, I always write, "Serve with Passion," and I mean it. Passion can't be contained; it's meant to be shared! So don't ever hold back from asking someone to help guide you. Most often, they will be honored and happy that you trust them enough to risk explaining your needs, even your weaknesses, the things you *don't* know. As you go through life, look for opportunities to "Pay it forward" and be a mentor to those seeking your advice. I really think that is what God put us on this earth to do.

Several years ago, my son Brent came to me and said he was interested in going into dental practice management. I happened to be good friends with Kerry Straine, one of the country's top dental practice management consultants located in Sacramento, California. Kerry agreed to set up a conference call with Brent about what it takes to go into the management side of dentistry.

"You really won't ever be totally confident about what you do until you've been in the business for ten years," Kerry said. "But I'll tell you what I'm willing to do, Brent. I've never done this before in the 30 years I've been doing this, but I'm going to be your personal coach and mentor for an entire year."

We couldn't believe it! Now, years later, Brent and I chuckle that in one phone call, Brent had become the Karate Kid and found his Mr. Miyagi in Kerry Straine. The ultimate, total expert and number one dental management consultant in America was willing to teach the newcomer.

Kerry was smart about how he approached it, and it's a good lesson for anyone willing to become a mentor. Kerry said, "Every Monday, Vera, my administrative assistant, will email you new information to study. On Thursdays, I'll jump on the phone to discuss it with you. If I'm not available, Vera will walk you through that week's session. And you are welcome to come to any seminar or program I am holding anywhere in the country at no cost."

Kerry did it the right way. He expressed his enthusiasm to help, but he clearly explained how much time he had, how he would use it, and what he expected from Brent.

Finally, he did something very important: he put boundaries on the arrangement—in this case, one year.

This time limit is important. What would be more demoralizing, or create a more searing memory, than to have your mentor just drift away or stop communicating without explanation?

So, remember: if you are the person being mentored, you have the burden of the other person's time and goodwill on your shoulders. Respect it.

A SHORT CHECKLIST FOR A BUSY MENTOR

- Set a clear understanding of how often you will be available and when
- Ask the mentee for a focused explanation of what they expect to learn from you
- Draw up a tight, cohesive study / action plan to accomplish the goals
- Have a staff member who can fill in when you are unavailable
- If you cannot be a mentor for an open-ended period of time, set clear boundaries on how long you can mentor (is it weeks, months, or a year or more)

At the risk of saying it again, don't hesitate to reach out and ask for help. It's the single most important thing you can do for your business, your career, your future. In an earlier chapter, I wrote about my crazy idea to write a letter to a motivational keynote speaker, author and consultant T. Scott Gross about my ideas for improving the healthcare industry by delivering great customer service. The end result was that we co-authored a book called *The Service Prescription, Healthcare the Way it was Meant to Be.*

So many people draw back from seeking mentors because they think the people they approach will reject them or make some humiliating excuse. The fact is that all of us—including me—are honored to be asked to mentor. When you have struggled up the mountain yourself and found success, there is awesome satisfaction in stretching out your hand and being able to help the courageous but struggling climber behind you. You know he has faced many of the same challenges as you have, and maybe he is just one step behind.

Ready to move your business from a dream to your destiny?
- List the people who could help you:
- Well-known "names" in your town or city who share your profession
- Effective leaders in your neighborhood, business district, place of worship

CALL TO ACTION:

What's your dream? _____

What's one step you could take TODAY to bring you closer to

your dream? _____

If you could pick a mentor to help, what profession would he/

she be in? _____

Have you looked for a mentor in local professional

organizations like:

Chamber of Commerce ____ Rotary clubs ____

Toastmasters_____

Weekly and monthly meetings of business and civic leaders

often held in:

In large local churches _____ libraries ____

organizations such as YMCA _____

Make a personal contact with one person involved in any three

of the above entities, and ask them for suggestions of meetings,

organizations. Take the next step, and be there.

CHAPTER FIVE

TEN INGREDIENTS TO
IGNITE THE SPARK

When people ask me to tell my life story—how I grew my business from a 1,100 square foot house, built in 1951 opposite a cow pasture to a multi-location business—I often get a reaction that goes something like this:

"Wow, Dr. Ayers, I know you've worked hard for everything, but you sure were lucky to be in the right place at the right time." What they really are trying to justify to themselves is this: "I could have done the same thing. If only I wasn't sidetracked by this-that-and-the-other-thing, I would have liked to have built a business like you did!"

Of course, I smile and try to say something encouraging. Inside I'm thinking, "If only they knew."

The truth is, I had a lot of "yesterdays" that could have haunted my path if I'd let them. The difference between the if-only folks and me was this: I took the new day at its word. I got up that day and *chose* to begin life as if it was brand new. Because—literally—it is.

Remember my mentor, Jack Bogart? I vividly recall discussing with him a situation that had happened at the office that had been seriously weighing me down. In many ways, it had paralyzed me. He looked me straight in the eyes and said his own version of the phrase at the beginning of this chapter.

———

Yesterday ended last night.
What matters right now is what's going on today.

———

"What happened yesterday is a canceled check…What might occur tomorrow is a promissory note…The only thing that matters is what you are going to do **today**." After many hours of observing and interviewing successful individuals and corporate CEOs, I've come to realize that they possess one quality above all that separates them from the person content to live with mediocrity.

———

The person who is achieving their dreams knows the power
of each day to change everything.

———

Your life is a choice that you have control over. If you take this truth to heart, the next time you look at a glass filled to the halfway mark, you'll optimistically see the glass as half-full versus half-empty. We all know people who see the world through a negative lens. You might say, "Beautiful day out today. Don't you think?" They reply, "Kind of overcast and gloomy to me." Those people can suck the life out of you. That's not to say I don't get down myself. I often allow negative circumstances to influence my day, too. I've just programmed my brain not to let the blahs take up residence there.

As a young man, I never would have found success in life if I had stayed fixated on my fractured leg and the end of my youthful dream to become a professional golfer. Don't get me wrong; there were plenty of grim days when I woke up close to giving up. Here's the difference: *I didn't.* That may sound simple, but ultimately, it's the difference between success and mediocrity. Remember this, write it down, and stick it in your pocket: "All sunshine and no rain makes a desert."

History is full of all the great inventors, entrepreneurs, corporate CEOs, and individuals who changed the world: Martin Luther King, Jr., Thomas Edison, Albert Einstein, and Mother Teresa, to name a few. I can assure you that they faced many failures and hardships prior to breaking through and making their mark in this world.

People content with being average quit searching; they abandon the dream that never materialized. If you resolve to stay focused and keep moving forward, you *will* find a path opening up that will lead you closer to your dream. It may not be the first dream you had in mind. You may have to make some realistic course corrections along the way. Remember: "Hold on; it's too soon to quit!"

You can't press on toward your goal if you are constantly looking in the rearview mirror.

Sometimes it's the side trail that turns out to be the route you were hoping to find, but you didn't know it. When I broke my leg and spent two months in traction in a hospital, followed by six months in a body cast, that horrible event forced me to think seriously about what career to pursue next.

———

**Dwelling on what happened yesterday is like
falling in quicksand.
That's when you get trapped and start sinking.**

———

What separates leaders and successful people from average people who struggle to take a leap of faith and go after their dreams but never quite manage to? Let's say there are ten ingredients that make up the recipe for success. The number "ten" is arbitrary; you could pick ten or 20 ingredients. The point is there are identifiable core components for building success. Here are ten of mine.

1. Successful people <u>have</u> dreams, but <u>act</u> on goals. A dream without a plan is a wish list.

The first ingredient of success is to have clearly defined goals. Successful people know how to harness the power of their dreams. They do that by strapping those dreams around clearly defined goals. Put it this way: your dream is the vision. It's *where you want to end up.* Dreams are the big, glorious things that feed your soul and keep you motivated to seek success. Goals are different. They are the workhorses of success. They slog along every day, looking at options, staying alert for obstacles, and adapting to circumstances that pop up along the way. You need the discipline of a goal—an actual roadmap— to achieve your dreams. It may be as simple as writing down three things you need to accomplish today and doing it! Congratulations. You're one step closer to achieving your dreams!

People who confuse their dreams and goals find it difficult to move forward because it's difficult to separate *what you want from what you need*. That's where mentors come in. They see the big picture because they aren't invested in your dreams. Dreaming is your job. Their job is to get you there.

**Dreams are abstract. Goals are concrete.
Your success is built on both.**

The eight months of lying on my back recuperating gave me ample time to think. I realized that to achieve my dream of becoming a dentist, I needed to make a list of goals that I had to reach to move me closer to the finish line. The first goal was making the mental commitment to do whatever it would take to go back to college, knowing that my study habits had to change drastically from what they were before. You've got to, for lack of a better word, become tunnel visioned in reaching the goals you have set.

In order for me to get into a position to take the Dental Aptitude Test (DAT), which is the entrance exam that all applicants around the country have to take, I first had to take all the required basic science and core courses required to take the exam. To be completely transparent with you, there were quite a few all-nighters while I crammed for organic chemistry, physics, and biochemistry exams. During those sleepless nights, my brain started playing games with my mind: "There is an easier way out, you know. You could change majors and relax and get into a less challenging degree without all the studying and stress that comes from sleep deprivation…all you have to do is QUIT!" My dream of becoming a dentist was so far down the road that all the goals that I had to accomplish to get there started to cloud my thinking. Having mentors that I could call at any hour, any time, was invaluable in getting me through those tough times.

When you set small concrete goals and achieve them, celebrate your success! It might be something as simple as taking your spouse, boyfriend, or girlfriend out to Starbucks because, starting tomorrow, you're one day closer to your dream! It's time to set and accomplish your next goal.

Words and feelings cannot express how it felt when I received my acceptance letter notifying me that I had been accepted to dental school. That sense of accomplishing that goal was and still is permanently etched in my mind! The dream that was etched in my brain in my preteen years was finally accomplished four years later. What a journey it was to finally walk across the stage and be handed my dental degree! About a week following graduation, I received a call from Uncle Fred letting me know how proud he was of my accomplishment. Then he said, "OK, now what. Where do we go from here?" To be perfectly honest with you, I was stunned by his statement. I thought to myself, "Do you have any idea what I've gone through to accomplish my dream? I've made it, mission accomplished!" Was I in for a rude awakening! Uncle Fred informed me that reaching your dreams isn't a destination but an ongoing journey. You never rest on the laurels of "I've arrived, so it's time to kick back and put my life on cruise control!" I often wonder if Uncle Fred even had cruise control installed in his car.

He said, "You are either going forward or falling backward. There is no middle ground!" Great advice! Entrepreneurs keep moving the bar forward. They utilize curiosity and perseverance, creativity, and open-mindedness to intentionally build the dream lives they want. When you hit your target, that's how you know it's time to get back in your present-day "sandbox" and plan your next dream!

What mentors like Uncle Fred and Jack Bogart defined for me was the fact those ideas were possible tactics– "But Greg, what's your goal?" That question forced me to think in concrete terms, and that's when I sat down with my staff and team and set the goals in concrete. "We're not here to sell a crown or a root canal or a dental implant or a teeth cleaning. We're here to sell a product called service excellence." Now, what does that look like, and what goals do we need to accomplish to produce it?

My mentors kept me focused on my goal—to deliver service excellence. All my other questions were answered over time and in the natural growth of my business. The most important thing was that the client base expanded as people responded enthusiastically to our welcoming, patient-first experience.

**You don't have to be smart at everything.
Just be smart enough to hang around smart people.**

Advertise? It turned out we didn't have to because patients found us. Move to a bigger building and hire more people? Sure, but not just any building or any staff—they had to reflect the goals and culture of the organization, which by then, with the help of mentors and my own resolve, I had clearly identified as service excellence.

2. Successful people serve with passion. It's the salt and seasoning of success.

I always sign the first book I co-authored, *The Service Prescription, Healthcare the Way It Was Meant to Be,* with three simple words: "Serve with Passion." If you don't have that fire in your belly to succeed, no dream or goal can possibly lift you high enough, or carry you far enough, to get you there. What I'm saying is, don't pay lip service to what you do— mean it! Have you ever been around a person who is passionate about what they do? It's contagious!

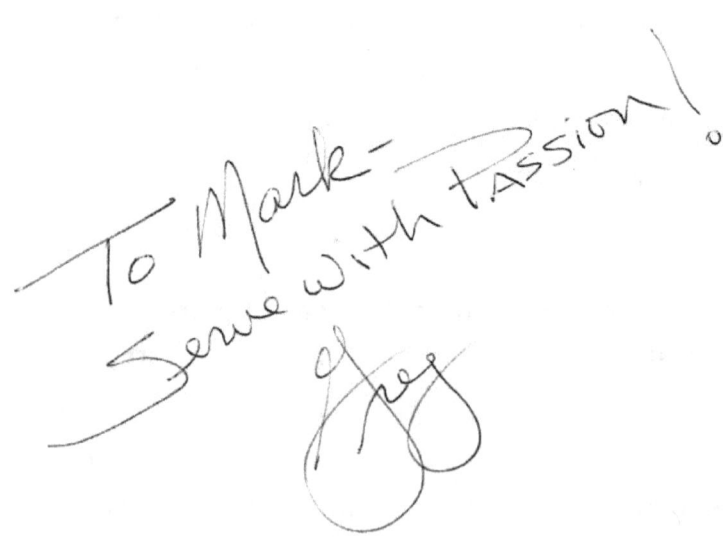

The great thing about passion is that it's not a quality that's limited to people with experience, special skills, or seven figures in the bank. Passion is open to everyone! The guy who gets his first job as a dishwasher can possess as much passion for work and getting ahead as the CEO of a Fortune 500 company. In fact, that's how many famous people literally rose from dishwasher to CEO; celebrity chefs and restaurant titans Bobby Flay and Emeril Lagasse, to name just two.

Serve with Passion
Skills are learned
Experience is earned
But passion comes from inside of you

Passion is important for many reasons. It keeps you going when times get tough. It's contagious. People are attracted to this quality in others and want to build on it. It's a quality that makes people fun and easy to be around; a person with passion gives off a lot of energy. I've said this before, but it bears repeating: **If you love what you do, you'll never have to work another day in your life.**

3. Successful people know when to let go.

Life is made up of daily choices strung out over time. Not every choice works out. Some years ago, I was at an age when the practice was doing very well, and I could start thinking about a future that included a comfortable retirement. To set it in motion, I sold half of my practice to a small group of dentists. At the time, it felt like a reasonable way to expand the business. They saw the opportunity to join a very successful practice, and I saw it as a way to start sharing the fruits of my labors—and the pressures of the business—while working with a group of good young dentists.

For many reasons, this partnership didn't work out as I had hoped. It turned out that we valued service in very different ways. That happens sometimes. Business partners can start out thinking they are on the same page and then change their habits, develop different goals, or just realize they aren't a good match after all. After spending months with everyone frustrated and in conflict, I realized that there was only one way forward. One day, I walked into our regular partner's meeting and said, "Guys, here's my letter of resignation. I'm going to be stepping down as the senior partner. I wish you all the best of luck."

_____

To get unstuck, first, you've got to let go.

_____

Letting go is not a panacea: "Gee, I just quit; now everything's great!" In fact, that was a very low period in my life. Everything I had created from the ground up, suddenly, had evaporated.

And it was the best thing that could have happened to me.

4. Successful people aren't afraid to try again.

If I hadn't let go, healed my wounds, and then tried again, the rest of the story—and this book—never would have happened.

Wounds? You bet. Life can hurt. It isn't a fairytale. But winning only comes to those who stay on the path despite all odds. Persistence means looking for interesting side trails and unexpected new vistas ahead because, eventually, they *will* appear.

———

Setbacks and blows can make one's judgment go helter-skelter for a while.
Take time to recover and examine what happened.
Analyze how to avoid those pitfalls again.

———

I can't sugarcoat it. At first, I was reeling, and I had to sit down in the middle of my path and nurse my wounds. My successful business was now in the hands of others. For a while, my thinking went like this. "That's it. I don't need this aggravation of building another business. I've already worked hard enough to build a good nest egg for my family and me." In effect, I was saying, "Go away and leave me alone!"

But that's OK. The worst thing you can do after a setback is to shove the injury inside you and let it fester. Better to step back a while, sit down on the path, be quiet, and make no big decisions. Let yourself heal.

Over time, I examined all aspects of the dissolved partnership and analyzed how I could avoid another one. Had I been too eager to change my circumstances and failed to sufficiently vet my prospective partners? Should I have approached our problems differently? These and other questions, while painful at first, became a valuable learning experience.

At just the right time, my sons Brent and Blake stepped in and suggested a new way of looking at things.

"C'mon, Dad, you're too young to retire! Let's build a new dental organization based on what made your old business so successful and use all the techniques and beliefs that you've preached all these years about great customer service.

"But this time, let's take it to a higher level. Let's really drill down into what makes an exceptional business dedicated to serving our patients. Let's research great companies and learn from all the best corporate advisors what it takes to build lasting success based on what you learned first from Uncle Fred about exceptional service. Let's build a company that will finally be the great legacy you deserve!"

Well, their words were like throwing gas on the fire for me. About all I could say was, "Man, that's awesome! Let's go!"

And we did.

First, I had to throw into the mix every ingredient for success that I believe in and am sharing with you now. We had to set new goals. We had to truly "let go" by banishing any bitterness over the past, since bitterness only slows you down. And we had to move forward with *passion*—the confidence and positive spirit that keeps the juice flowing to overcome every challenge. Only then could we jumpstart a new dream.

———

Today's defeat makes future success all the sweeter.

———

Our first challenge was the location. Because I had a non-compete agreement with my former partners, we had to rebuild about 35 miles away in two little towns, Woodruff and Boiling Springs. So, we bought two old, dilapidated practices. Honestly, both offices should have been shut down by the health department, but we bought them anyway. It was amazing how hard and focused work transformed those little hovels.

Brent was as energized as me, and we quickly determined that our interests harmonized well together. He was interested in the dental management side of the business, and through our research into great companies and consultants, he quickly found amazing opportunities to grow professionally. As noted before, he found a mentorship with the highly-respected dental management consultant Kerry Straine and was invited to join a consultant roundtable group with the John Maxwell organization.

Together, we began to grow a new business, and sure enough, it took off. What attracted customers, new and old, was our commitment to use all my experience—passion supplied by not only Brent but all my family—to build a culture and a new business totally devoted to customer service.

That's how ProGrin Dental was born.

So, do you think I was glad to start over again?!

5. Say No To the Naysayers.

There are many reasons people will try to convince you *not* to do something. It's pretty easy to figure out who the naysayers are. They are either stuck in fearful mediocrity or simply can't stand to see someone else take risks and succeed. Of course, sometimes those who say "no" to you will do so for a valid reason that's temporary or based on faulty information. That's why giving up and "taking no for an answer" should never be an option.

We're all inspired by the great stories of amazing people who started out rejected, turned down, fired, or destitute—but never gave up.

Walt Disney was fired from the Kansas City Star in 1919 because his editor reportedly said he "lacked imagination and had no good ideas." Albert Einstein was expelled from school; ground-breaking comedian Jerry Seinfeld was fired from his first sitcom; and Marilyn Monroe was advised to forget Hollywood and become a secretary. As a young TV reporter, Oprah Winfrey's bosses criticized her for being too "empathetic" with the people she interviewed. Two men who will go down in history as technology giants each knew the sting of defeat: Bill Gates's first software business failed, and Steve Jobs was fired from his own company.

———

Basketball great Michael Jordan reportedly said:
"I have missed over 9,000 shots in my career. I have lost almost 300 games. On 26 occasions, I was expected to take the game-winning shot and missed. I have failed over and over again in my life.
And that is why I succeed."

———

The comeback story of Colonel Sanders is also a great lesson. He was forced to power through many noes and naysayers before he founded Kentucky Fried Chicken. I like his story because he was a skilled and successful entrepreneur several times over, but he still suffered many professional defeats beyond his control. Yet he never quit. He started out poor and had to take a slew of jobs to support himself, including work as an insurance salesman and gas station manager.

The first business he built himself was a motel which became very successful, and it only failed because World War II sapped the economy and his customers vanished. So, he started a restaurant to sell a tasty chicken recipe he had developed. He was doing great business until the early 1950s, when an interstate highway was built that diverted his customers down another route. His restaurant location became a dead-end street.

Suddenly, he was unemployed, 65 years old, and living on a $105 per month Social Security check. White-haired, maybe, but he was determined! Colonel Sanders set off around the country trying to get restaurants to buy his recipe for amazingly tasty chicken. Many of the restaurant owners he met laughed at him. One man, Pete Harmon, a friend, gave him a chance, and an iconic American brand was on its way.

What if these men and women had listened to the naysayers? You get the idea.

6. Successful people never stop learning.

People who are passionate about learning are living in the *now*. They are aware and alive. In many ways, I believe my youthful commitment to do something special with my life grew out of my hunger to *learn*. I realized that new information isn't threatening but empowering. There's no way to conquer obstacles and move forward with your dreams unless you're willing to take in new ideas and challenge your current thinking.

**Learning: the lifeblood of success
It motivates you to see new possibilities.
Serves as a technical resource to grow professionally with new skills, and builds confidence through personal self-improvement.**

Once again, I stress the importance of mentors. They are the people who challenge you, open your mind, and make you think about things in a fresh light.

Sometimes their counsel is painful and hard to hear. That makes them even more valuable! Mentors can be personal advisors who come out of your circle of professionals or from your city or region— and sometimes, they're your own Uncle Fred. For the ultimate online mentor experience, I go back again and again to the TED conferences for insights and enlightenment; the entire TED organization is designed to distribute "ideas worth spreading." The organization sponsors online and in-person conferences all over the world featuring top motivators and "up-and-coming world changers." But you don't have to necessarily become a "TEDster" to learn. A little research will reveal multitudes of motivational speakers, books, and conferences that personally speak to you and can help you take your next step.

Learning is essential as a technical resource. If you want to find true, lasting, and satisfying success, you should aspire to be a leader in the industry—even if it's just in your hometown.

That means growing in knowledge and skills, and that's why continuing education is essential. Sadly, I know classmates of mine whose practices are still based on the four years of education they had 35 years ago. While it's true in every profession, in my neck of the woods—dentistry—continuing education is the frontier of new ideas. Without new dental technology, we'd still be pulling out teeth with pliers and hand-dipping X-rays into the processor! Seriously, the rise of laser dentistry, digital x-rays, implant procedures, and advances in cosmetic dentistry has changed the profession. It's likely that there are new improvements, technologies, and ideas in your profession coming at lightning speed. Unless you take advantage of them, you will be left behind.

Learning builds personal and professional confidence. I seized an opportunity to attend a Dale Carnegie course, which has for decades been a resource for people who want to thrive in their professional and personal lives. The course stresses human-relations skills and how to build rewarding relationships. It's been invaluable in deepening my interactions with patients, employees, and colleagues. In my case, I had no idea that building a successful practice would lead to so many opportunities to reach out to others. In recent years, Brent and I have arranged many conference groups in response to the many young professionals who come to me asking, "How did you build your successful practice?" Other groups, like business organizations and book clubs, are always eager to hear how a person has "made it." Be ready for those opportunities to share your story.

Visit companies that promote values you admire. I like to point out to my team that companies have personalities like people do. Chick-fil-A has a corporate culture that reflects our belief in putting the customer first. Greeting people with a smile while looking them in the eye. That's making a statement! We all learn from others. In Chapter 3, I explained how I concocted the "Three Restaurants" lesson to show my team in real time how differences in customer service affected their perceptions. Sometimes the best learning isn't in a classroom; it's in real life. Use it.

Seize the day! Keep learning. People who are stuck in the past get passed over.

---

7. Successful people know how to inspire their team.

You found your dream by yourself. You set your goals with the help of a few others. But you will not fully succeed until you pass everything on to your entire team.

When Brent and I founded ProGrin Dental, we decided to reinforce our culture of service excellence by holding a Vision Day in the spring and fall for our entire dental organization. It was an opportunity to immerse them in our company's vision of putting our patients first and promoting a culture where each person on staff aspires to be the very best. The first thing on the agenda was to communicate the importance of passion and enthusiasm. One of the first things I say is, "Listen, I'm not hiring you for your skills. I'm hiring *you.*"

Your dream is inside you.
Your success is determined by the people you keep around you.

Thanks to our Vision Days, we have assembled a team of trustworthy and confident employees who know our vision of exceptional customer service and how to carry it out. Employees don't pick up your vision by telepathy. It's up to you to inspire them.

We start with the first incoming telephone call. Our employees are so well trained that they know deep in their bones what to do even in an emergency.

For example, if a parent calls, frantic and in tears, to say that her eight-year-old Little Leaguer has just been hit in the mouth with a baseball, do you think our receptionist takes the time to scan the computer schedule to find a convenient open time for them to come to the office?

Are you kidding? Instead, she says, "How soon can you be here?" In those six words, my valued employee knew what it means when I say, *"Serve with passion."*

8. Successful people attract the best.

Not long ago, Brent and I met at the end of a long day to grab a quiet dinner at a steak and seafood house close to one of our new offices. The minute our server appeared, we could tell right away she was going to make our evening better. She had a welcoming smile and an alert way of greeting us which enhanced the dining experience. First, she noticed I had on a ProGrin Dental scrub. She said, "Oh! You're a dentist! I'm just finishing dental assisting school!"

This young woman radiated health and energy. When she left with our order, I said to Brent, "There's an exceptional young lady. I think she should work for us." The next day, Brent went back to talk to her and got more information. It turned out Keri wasn't sure she was cut out to be a dental assistant; what attracted her was the opportunity to be in a profession that brought people genuine satisfaction and confidence since she knew the value of a healthy and beautiful smile.

Brent saw beyond her hesitation over the technical side of dentistry. "She's got a great attitude," he told me. "She'd be great in management."

We offered her a job to grow with ProGrin Dental, and she seized it. Now Keri is on our management team. She is both sharp in the business side of things and compassionate about what we do and how we treat our team and patients.

Success depends on staying alert: Keep your eyes open for quality people.

---

9. Successful people value their mistakes as much as their triumphs.

Everyone enjoys hearing the story of Thomas Edison because he teaches the great value of failure to a magnificent degree. According to historical records, Edison, after drifting away from other jobs, made a thousand unsuccessful attempts at inventing the light bulb. Some versions of the story put his attempts at ten thousand. What matters is how Edison responded to failure. "I didn't fail a thousand times," he famously said. "The light bulb was an invention with a thousand steps."

Talk about steely-eyed hard-headedness! In fact, Edison was an expert at failing. He held more than a thousand patents, and not one was perfected on the first try. Once, someone commented on his nine thousand tries to invent a type of storage battery, saying, "Too bad you have no results." Edison reportedly replied, "Results! Why, man, I have gotten lots of results! I know several thousand things that won't work!"

———

It's OK to bury your failures and mistakes.
In fact, they are your foundation and fertilizer for future success.

———

No doubt about it, there is a strange but powerful relationship between success and failure. You cannot have one without the other. Celebrate success, but learn to embrace your mistakes and failures, too, because somewhere in those murky depths are the seeds of a fresh beginning.

10. The Golden Rules of Business.

*Treat others as you would want to be treated.
*Catch your employees doing something right vs. always looking for them to be doing something wrong.

*Compliment your employees in front of your customers/patients.

*When you make a mistake, own up to it, and say you're sorry.

*Celebrate your successes.

*Look for opportunities to give your services away to those less fortunate, to first responders, and to the men and women in uniform who protect our great country.

*Listen more than you talk; there is a reason why God gave you two ears and one mouth.

*Jesus said it best when he said, "And whatsoever you do to the least of these, you do unto me."

CHAPTER SIX

THE "Y" IN THE ROAD: WHEN IT'S YOUR TURN TO MENTOR

When you get advice from someone you respect, the results can be unforgettable. That's why I'm so high on seeking out mentors. I want you to find your own Uncle Fred or Jack Bogart. Mentors open the brain and drop things inside that could take years to learn if you tried to figure it out for yourself.

And sometimes, the mentor you're looking for is staring back at you in the mirror.

One of the most rewarding things you can do in life is reach behind you and pull someone else forward. When you pass on what you know and what you've learned—especially to a young person— you may have set their course for the rest of their lives.

My son and business partner, Brent, and I believe this so strongly that we began a special leadership program for adults and young people in upstate South Carolina. We hosted a seminar each year from one of our mentors, John Maxwell, so that others in our community could attend his world-acclaimed leadership conference called Live 2

Lead. We invited business leaders, church leaders, community leaders, and first responders from around the region. It was an opportunity to give back and train others to become better leaders in their workplace and community.

The response was amazing. Over 300 attended the first year, and every year since, the event continues to grow. We decided to open the event to teenagers and share with them at a young age the building blocks that great leaders possess. It was like turning on a lightbulb. Their response and enthusiasm were contagious. It inspired us to use what we do, dentistry, as a platform to develop tomorrow's leaders "One Smile at a Time."

POP TEACHES A HARD LESSON

One of the most influential men in my life was my grandfather, Marion Lee Ayers. He had a stellar career in the newspaper business, serving as publisher of several newspapers. In fact, back in the 1950s, he was offered the role of publisher of *The New York Times* and politely turned it down. He also was elected by his peers to serve as President of the Democratic Press Association. I remember seeing pictures in his office of him meeting with Presidents Truman and Eisenhower in the White House Oval Office.

He taught me a profound life lesson during my freshman year of college when I was playing on a golf scholarship. One lesson especially has stayed with me.

At the time, I'm sure I was an over-confident kid thinking that I had life figured out playing college golf and making decent grades. I called Pop up one afternoon with a special request. I needed to borrow $100 to buy the latest and greatest Power Built graphite shaft golf driver. He told me to come on over.

When I stopped by his place that afternoon, he was sitting at his desk. I made myself comfortable in his black leather chair. We engaged in some small talk, catching him up on the results of my recent chemistry exam. He was my biggest, raving fan! Having made it to the pinnacle of his profession, he always encouraged me to go after my dreams.

He reached over on his desk and handed me an envelope with a check made out to Greg Ayers for $100.00. Wanting to impress him with my mature business savvy, I reached over and took a legal pad and wrote this:

I, Gregory Lee Ayers, promise to pay Marion T. Ayers, $100. Signed, Greg Ayers
Date: 10-12-1973

My first business transaction ever and who better to impress and do it with than my grandfather?! I knew he would be proud of me. After I handed him the IOU, he held it in his hand for what seemed like an unusually long time, staring at the simple one-sentence legal document I had just drafted. He twirled around in his office chair and tossed the document on his desk, kind of like one would do tossing a frisbee. He then spun around and asked if he could see the $100 check he had just given me. Not knowing what to expect, I pulled the check out of my pocket and handed it back to him. He proceeded to rip it up into what seemed like a thousand pieces and tossed it into the trash can under his desk.

As I sat there in shock, not knowing what to say, he spun around and looked me right in the eyes, leaned over, and placed his finger on the tip of my nose, and said, "You asked me if I would loan you one hundred dollars this morning, which implies that you will pay it back. That piece of paper means nothing to me. Your word, your name, your character are what counts to me! If that piece of paper has more value than your word and good name, then you're not worth a damn!"

At that point, Pop had only whacked the ball. Now he followed through with a homerun that took it out of the ballpark. "Greg, listen to me carefully. The most important thing you have in life is your good name. You can either live up to your good name, or you can screw it up, and if you do screw it up, you probably have ruined your name for life."

I never got that $100 from my grandfather, but in a way, that check has stayed with me for my whole life. In one afternoon, Pop passed on to an overconfident young adult a universal life lesson that I have shared with my four sons and countless friends and acquaintances, including you, over the past 40 years.

———

Integrity: Doing the right thing
Even when no one is watching,
And there is nothing in writing to catch you

———

SHOWING THE WAY

It's amazing how much influence you can have on someone just by being there and offering quiet, persistent encouragement to turn dreams into concrete action.

Daniel has been my patient since he was in grade school. He was a great kid, raised by a single mom. When he'd come into the office for a checkup, I'd always take time to chat with him, starting with the classic, "What do you want to be when you grow up?"

"I want to be a pilot," Daniel said.

"That's quite a goal!" I'd say. "I always wanted to fly, too. How do you think you're gonna make it happen?"

We talked about how, when he got to a certain age, he could start building on his dreams.

Sure enough, one day, years later, when he was a teenager, Daniel came in for a checkup, and I was very interested to know how life was going for him.

"Hey, Dr. Ayers. I'm old enough now to take flying lessons!" he said.

"No way! Man, that's amazing!" I said.

Next thing you know, Daniel is back again—I don't think he even needed a dental checkup—but he came in on his own time with exciting news. He was scheduled to take his solo flight on his 16th birthday, no less.

I was so proud of him, and I think my support meant something to him, too. Daniel went to school and studied aeronautical engineering and went on to fulfill his dream to the fullest. Today, he is a pilot with Delta Airlines, and every so often, he texts me photos of himself in the cockpit and tells me about his latest jaunt.

Every time I hear from Daniel, I am thrilled to think how this young man took a dream and didn't allow anyone to crush it. It makes me happy to know I played a role in encouraging his journey. In fact, I consider it a privilege, and it continues to this day. Without question, I'm confident that Daniel will be an encouraging mentor to some young person looking to pursue their dreams.

———

**A mentor's reminder to a young dreamer: Dreams are the fuel that ignites success.
Goal setting and persistence are the sparks that fire the launch.**

———

DROPPING THE BATON

Not every dream ends well. There was an incident involving the USA Olympic 4x100 men's relay team that became famous because it was so heartbreaking. Understand that these men were the four fastest runners in the world. The team was positioned to take the gold. The baton was passed to the next guy in line. However, as the third member of the relay team was passing the baton to the last runner, the unthinkable occurred; they dropped the baton! They were disqualified, so they did not walk away with the gold medal.

Everyone watching wondered how the best of the best could drop the baton. They could have dropped their heads with embarrassment and refused to run their next race, but they made a choice: they were going to review the film second by second and see where the mistakes were made and practice the handoff over and over to assure that it wouldn't happen again. Then they went out there and won.

Understand that we all will drop the baton at times in our lives. That's just life. It's how we respond and refuse to throw in the towel that separates winners from losers.

Sometimes as a mentor, you will be drawn into a person's disappointments and failures—those moments when they dropped the baton. Don't pull back. That's when mentorship is most critical.

I had the honor of supporting another young man through just such a critical juncture. I'll call him Cody. Cody was a real self-starter. In fact, he didn't need any coaxing to jumpstart his dreams. I was impressed with his confidence because he came to me on his own to ask if he could shadow me for a while. He thought he wanted to be a dentist. The thing was, he had already earned a degree in another field, so he was basically starting over again, taking all the required college science classes necessary to apply to dental school. I was glad to help, but in the back of my mind, I wondered if he was truly committed to following a new career or was he one of those people who gets jazzed by dreams but is never motivated to follow through.

"What do I have to do to get into dental school?" he asked me.

My advice was to talk to the Dean of Admission first, to start at the beginning and make sure it was what he wanted. He did that and applied. *And he didn't get in.*

The next year, he applied again, and once again, he was denied a place in the upcoming class. I felt for him because, of course, it was embarrassing. I also knew that no one needs a good mentor more than when he or she is facing failure.

I shared with Cody my own experience prior to going before the admissions committee years before. At the time, I was really struggling. The car accident that shattered my leg shattered my athletic dreams along with it, and after that, my college studies had really gone downhill. I, too, had to take the admissions test a second time. So, I was ready when the question came during my interview from a faculty member on the admissions committee: "So, Greg, what are you going to do when you don't get into dental school this year?"

It's kind of a trick question, but it's a valuable one, too. The way you answer it is a litmus test of the strength of your dream and your determination. If your answer is, "Well, if I don't get in, I'm probably going to be a biology teacher somewhere." You can pretty much bet you're going to be a biology teacher somewhere!

But if you really and truly want to be a dentist, the correct answer is: "If I don't get in, I'm going back to figure out *why* I failed, and I'm gonna correct that and try again. I may never be at the top of the class in raw numbers, but *nobody* is gonna beat me in passion and drive!"

That's how I answered the committee, and that's how I advised Cody. It was up to him to figure out which he wanted to be—a biology teacher or a dentist.

***

Mentors are the most valuable when they show the value of failure.

***

Cody figured it out. After three failed attempts, he finally succeeded and gained acceptance to dental school, and we all celebrated with him. But that wasn't the end of the story because he still had challenges ahead.

The second year of dental school is the most grueling of all academically. There is so much material to learn—from all the basic science courses to all the dental classes and lab work— that you get loaded down, and it wears on you. In that second year, Cody called me and said, "Dr. Ayers, I just don't know if I can do this."

"Cody," I said, "you know how hard it was to get from point A to point B just to gain admission into dental school? That was a feat unto itself! You were so persistent, and you said, 'Nothing's gonna stop me.' You aren't giving up now, are you?"

I really pulled out all the stops. "If you stick it out, you'll have a lot of fun the last two years since that's when you're in the clinics and really learning how to become a dentist. But you gotta get there, buddy. After all you've been through, you don't want to be the guy who gave up on his dreams and ends up punching a clock somewhere."

The next thing I said may have been my finest hour as a mentor. It's risky to give the whole, unvarnished truth to a discouraged young person, but I had a feeling this would work. I said, "You know what, Cody? I'll level with you. There *is* no easier way. You're gonna have to work your butt off until you get through this. But once they hand you that degree, it's yours. They can never take it back, and your career is all yours unless you screw it up."

FINISH STRONG

After all he went through, it's a real pleasure to say that Cody became a dentist, and a good one. He married a young woman who is also a dentist, and they have a very successful practice near Atlanta.

Looking back, I'm prouder of this young man for his failures and determination than if he had sailed into dental school on the first try.

For all these reasons—from Uncle Fred to Pop; for Daniel, Cody and all the young people I've met and tried to encourage along the way—I'm convinced that we could motivate and energize many more young people if all of us who have been seasoned by life took the time to mentor *at least one of them.*

With so many aimless and lost young people today, it has occurred to me that, when it comes to mentoring, the old line "If it ain't broke, don't fix it" is definitely *not* true.

The fact is, many young people *need* to break things, to shake things up. They need *hope.* Mentors are the cheerleaders who say, "If it's not broke, figure out a way to break it and make something new." Think about it. If a person is serious about turning dreams into reality, *change is their biggest ally.* That's the only way to grow.

So as a mentor, develop a plan of action with each young person.

Teach them to try new things, one step at a time.

After all, that's how every 1,000-mile journey begins.

Five steps a mentor can suggest to young people to ignite their dreams

1. Find someone who is doing what you want to do. Call them up, and ask to visit. They will be honored that you asked, and if they aren't, let me know about it!

2. Go online, and find businesses, schools, organizations that speak to your interests. Research their websites and become knowledgeable about the issues they believe in. Be honest. Do they excite you enough to want to get more involved?

3. Look in the mirror. Is there <u>one thing</u> you can improve about yourself that makes you more "ready" to chase your dream? If it's an athletic endeavor, are you healthy and in good shape? If it's taking a public role, are you up-to-date in your appearance, have good diction, and confidence in public speaking? If it's using a skill (woodworking, a new language, a musical instrument) are you able to demonstrate a skill level that will help you get in the door?

4. Seek out apprenticeships and internships offered by businesses and organizations. Many seasoned professionals began that way.

5. Keep a digital recorder or a notebook to record your ideas and impressions about your goals as they mature and grow. As you meet people, shadow a pro, research career paths, you will be uncovering new ideas and paths that may take you in new and exciting directions.

CHAPTER SEVEN

THE WINNING PRESCRIPTION: DRILL IN FERTILE SOIL AND PLANT GOOD HABITS

Want to meet your goals and become a winner? For starters, follow what I call the chameleon rule: *you become who you hang around with*. You want to be a winner, so hang around winners. Plenty of people hang around losers. Prisons and unemployment lines are filled with them. But remember that **winning and losing aren't a place but a way of thinking**. Many people use the time being broke or in prison, to *change* their thinking, and many of them become the most amazing winners of all. History is filled with people who started out as walking human disasters. When they woke up and finally decided to contribute and make a difference for the good, they changed the world.

FINDING THAT FERTILE SOIL

I have this image in my head of a tree that's forced to grow in two kinds of soil. Half the roots are sunk in dusty, lifeless sand, but just on the other side of the tree is rich deep soil, and some of the roots have reached it. Half the tree is lifeless, and the other half is producing beautiful foliage and fruit.

People grow like that, too. Put them in a good environment, give them goals and the right people to hang around, and they thrive. Take away the fertile soil, surround them with poor role models, and many people become lifeless and starved of any purpose.

I have mentioned Og Mandino, the famous author and motivator, in previous sections, and I want to return to his story. Like our tree above, Og had a period in his life where he also was stuck in lifeless soil—to the extent he was thinking about actually ending his life—when something began rustling and kicking inside of him to get going and seek good soil. His way of doing that was to travel across the country to visit libraries and devour books on success. *He had no one but himself as a guide, but he became a success by seeking success.*

**If you want to be a winner,
your first responsibility is to seek the soil that will
make you grow.**

Those of us in leadership positions in organizations and businesses are also responsible for the kind of soil we make available to our employees and colleagues. Good soil will grow great organizations and businesses. Galatians 6:7 says, "Whatsoever a man soweth, that shall he also reap."

Of course, we can't control everything about our environment. Sometimes we're just in a lousy place, with no winners in sight. Then we have to deal with it. *We have to become our own winner first.*

No person proves that more than a remarkable guy named Shaka Senghor.

Senghor described his rise from convicted murderer to charismatic motivator in a TED talk he gave in 2014. His life is a powerful case study about the effect of bad and good soil and about hanging around losers *and* hanging around winners because he's done both. In his TED talk, he identifies the essential qualities of keeping goals and the powerful role of mentors.

As a kid, Senghor was an honor roll student with dreams of becoming a doctor. Those firm goals were shaken in his teen years when his parents divorced. Raised in a heavy-crime area of Detroit, Shaka was 17 when he was shot while standing on a street corner.

He didn't die, but the incident warped his thinking and destroyed his goals. He had no mentors, no dad, and no family members to keep him focused. When he got out of the hospital, he was embittered and tough. He vowed that from that day on, he would always be the shooter, never the victim. He became "a drug dealer with a quick temper and a semi-automatic pistol," and in 1991, he fulfilled his vow when he shot and killed a man.

Convicted of second-degree murder and facing decades in prison, Senghor describes himself as "bitter, angry, and hurt." He says, "I blamed everybody from my parents to the system." In prison, he went from bad to worse—"the worst of the worst"—and became a prison drug dealer. When he was caught, his side enterprise got him thrown in solitary confinement for more than seven years.

Talk about living in lifeless soil! Then, one day, Shaka Senghor got a letter from his young son—he didn't get many of those—that read: "Dad, don't kill. Jesus watches what you do. Pray to him."

"I am not religious, but there was something profound about that; it made me examine my life," Shaka said. He began to try to find a way to turn around his life. It wasn't easy to do in solitary confinement, but he did it.

His first task was to find great mentors—and yes, he found them among his fellow prisoners. Some were serving life sentences, but they wanted to make something of themselves. Inspirational outreaches like the Prison Project and Chuck Colson's Prison Fellowship recognize the value of finding good soil where you are. For many years, these organizations and ones like them have been helping prisoners develop meaningful lives behind bars.

One of Senghor's next steps was to begin writing a journal about his life. That led him to the idea of acknowledging he had hurt others, asking forgiveness, and atoning for his wrongs; in other words, trying to make up for the wrong he had done. He made a new vow, too; he vowed that if he ever were released from prison, he would do everything in his power to become the kind of man who would help others.

In 2010, after two decades of incarceration, Senghor reached his goal and walked out. Now he helps other ex-prisoners who are reentering society. He teaches at the University of Michigan and is involved in business enterprises and organizations that allow him to be a mentor to young people and guide them on the right path. Shaka Senghor has become the kind of mentor he wished he had in his life years before.

"Anybody can have a transformation if we create a space for that to happen."
-Shaka Senghor, TED Talk, March, 2014

What's more, he believes that most men and women who are incarcerated are redeemable like he was, "and we have a role in what kind of people they will be."

Shaka Senghor is living proof that much of our destiny is shaped by the losers and winners we hang with, but our first responsibility is to look in the mirror. If we choose to make the effort, it is possible to change the soil we find ourselves in.

It doesn't take a horticulturalist to scoop up a palm's worth of soil and know the difference between a handful that is dry and crumbling and a handful that's moist and loamy with nutrients. In an organization or a person, it's just as possible to tell the good soil from the bad. Health has a way of showing itself. There is an energy, a direction, and a sense of forward movement in both a person and a business that is healthy.

But how do you create the conditions to thrive in fertile soil?

One of the great college football coaches and a legend in my native state of South Carolina, Lou Holtz, knew how to answer that question on the football field. Interestingly enough, he also knew how to pick his soil; he knew that he thrived as a college coach and wasn't cut out for coaching in the pros. He didn't mind saying so, either. After resigning in the middle of a 3-10 losing season with the New York Jets, Holtz explained his decision by saying, "God did not put Lou Holtz on this earth to coach in the pros."

3 ways people and companies reveal their 'growth' pattern	
GROWING IN FERTILE SOIL	**STRUGGLING IN 'SAND'**
Shows a cheerful helpful public persona	Shows carelessness, lack of energy
Makes it a priority to focus the team, and individually, to foster personal growth and goal setting (e.g., journal writing, prayer, meditation, staying fit)	Appears unfocused, scattered: slow to fix problems, answer questions, reluctant to communicate, allows mistakes to fester or multiply.
Goes the extra mile to make sure customers, patients, colleagues, friends, family, are happy.	Shows lack of creativity in problem solving, in developing new ideas and ways to improve the status quo.

Holtz, now retired, was known as a great motivator, which is part of what makes a coach great. He had a way of expressing truths about life and becoming a winner that made people, and his teams, sit up and listen. He's known for a number of sayings. One of them—though we didn't take it from Holtz—is a good summary of the philosophy Brent and I followed when we founded ProGrin Dental:

My dear friend and dental mentor, Linda Miles, told me early on in my career *your attitude determines your altitude*—program yourself and your team to have a great day. Dr. Duane Schmidt from Cedar Rapids, IA, said this sentence at a seminar I attended over 30 years ago. It has stayed with me all these years: "I once decided to have a bad day…and I didn't like it." Even beyond skills and motivation, it's the right attitude that takes your dream, your idea, and your goals up to the next level. That means creating a culture, an environment, where exceptional service can grow.

———

"Ability is what you're capable of doing. Motivation determines what you do. Attitude determines how well you do it."
-Lou Holtz

———

TO PLANT IN FERTILE SOIL:

<u>Begin</u> by treating others as valued individuals.

<u>Follow through</u> by using 100% of your skills to meet their needs.

<u>Build a winning culture</u> by turning these good intentions into daily habits.

HABITS DETERMINE WHAT HAPPENS NEXT

Sure, some days it's easier to do good than others. All of us have lives away from the office. A child gets sick; a parent passes away; a vacation falls through; life happens to each of us. That's where good habits kick in and do their work. *Good habits are the workhorses that take over when you don't feel like lifting the load that day.*

You can't develop good habits in lousy soil. You always need to think about how you can keep the soil fertilized and watered—that is, motivated—so you can develop a conscious culture of winning.

ACTION PLAN:
<u>USE YOUR HABITS TO FORM A CONSCIOUS</u>
<u>CULTURE OF WINNING</u>

Hang with winners. Seek out people who already <u>are</u> where you want to <u>be.</u>

Review your goals every day and ask: *"How did my daily habits impact my goals?"*

-Which habits brought me closer today to my dream?
-Did I indulge in any habits that will steer me off course?
-What's one thing I can do <u>tomorrow</u> to reinforce a good habit or
  snap off a bad one?

Keep a journal of your goals, fears, frustrations, successes, and watch the pattern that develops over time. Even unconsciously, you are creating a roadmap for the way ahead.

In business, call each member of your team to accountability on a regular basis. Set specific goals, and reinforce them with encouragement and if necessary, correction.

Be honest. Don't forget to hold yourself accountable, too!

CHAPTER EIGHT

TAKING YOUR TEAM TO THE NEXT LEVEL

THE INVERTED TRIANGLE

The concept of developing a personal connection with your employees and recognizing their needs as a top business priority—even treating them like family—is not new.

However, in practice, it takes many different forms, which, in and of itself, suggests that the basic idea is sound.

Probably the most famous interpretation dates back to 1970 when a former AT&T executive, Robert Greenleaf, wrote an essay introducing the concept of a business owner/manager as a "servant leader." He rejected the authoritarian top-down style of business leadership and introduced the idea (put in general terms) that a healthy business is one in which employees' needs are considered first, and when they are given a reason to contribute through their work for the good of themselves, their company and society. Sounds pretty good, doesn't it?

The idea of managing from the ground up and making employees a top priority has grown in popularity and has been re-interpreted many times since Mr. Greenleaf's time.

Today, the modern versions all stress the concept that the organization is healthier when leadership recognizes that the well-being of their employees is essential to success.

At ProGrin Dental, we express this idea of "servant leadership," using what I like to call *inverting the triangle*—in other words, recognizing that businesses thrive when the owner/manager/CEO operates in the position of support, at the base of the triangle, with employees second in the tier and the customer at the top. It looks like this:

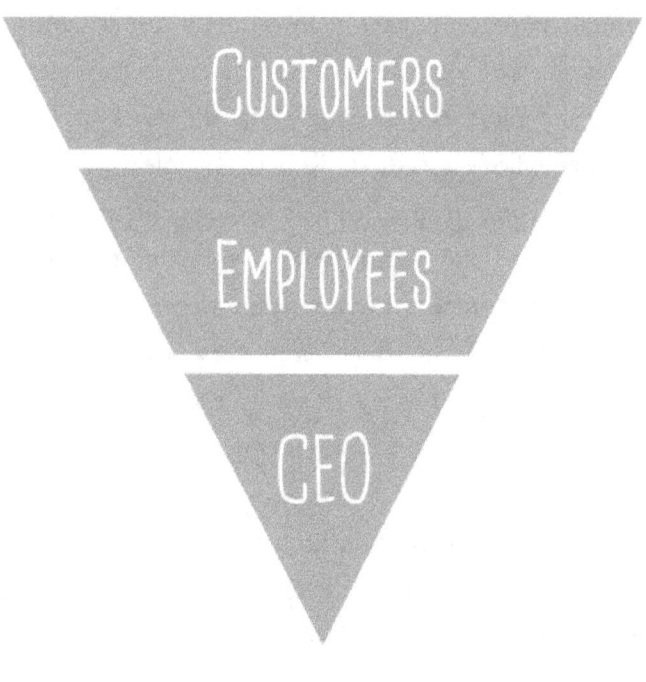

INVERTED TRIANGLE

CUSTOMERS

EMPLOYEES

CEO

The job of management is to empower its employees and to give them the necessary direction and resources to best serve those at the top of the inverted triangle: the customer. Yes, we use this model in the dentistry business, but it applies across all industries.

The organizational charts of old always portrayed corporate-level people at the top, with a very obvious trickle-down to the managers, supervisors, and then the men and women who do most of the work. There was never mention of the customer or client.

If you're in the corporate suite, you won't be there long if the folks answering to you aren't producing and being creative. Your job is to provide motivation, direction, and purpose. These activities support your employees. When employees feel supported, they begin to feel a sense of ownership. And when employees feel like the efforts are important, the customer or client notices. That's when positive things begin to happen. That is the essence of the inverted triangle.

THE CIRCLE OF INFLUENCE

As I mentioned earlier, when you empower and encourage your team to give excellent service or to create a superior product, that, in turn, encourages loyalty from customers, no matter the industry.

This is what I call the Circle of Influence (COI).

Your customers' demonstration of loyalty naturally attracts new customers who are also seeking either excellent service or a superior product. The circle is complete when your expanding customer base further empowers your team. It looks like this:

UNCLE FRED WAS THERE FIRST

At our company, our goal with the "inverted triangle" concept and the Circle of Influence is to give our employees incentives beyond money and benefits for wanting to work for us, with us, and, yes, for themselves, to create an exceptional customer experience.

In fact, it's both personally and professionally interesting to me how in tune Uncle Fred's instincts were back in the 1960s. He was already implementing 21st-century ideas when it came to emphasizing the importance of teamwork and taking his team to the next level.

As I noted in an earlier chapter, it was Uncle Fred who bought multiple cases of Og Mandino's books to give to his employees. He understood from his bones out to his skin that he needed to communicate his vision and inspiration to his team because, without them, his vision would soon go to black.

Here's another way to think about it. I like to call it a matter of being *employee conscious.*

Brent and I often meet with many aspiring dentists in the process of building their practice. When the talk turns to hiring young dentists, we want to talk first about finding the right hygienists and dental assistants. "Where do I look for the best candidates? How do I find the best people for my budget?" and so on.

"Of course, your technical team is critically important," I tell them. "But don't start there. Start with the people in your front office, with your receptionist."

A lot of our listeners look at me like, *"Say what?* You can find a good receptionist anywhere!"

That's when I say, "Wait a minute. Who is the first person to communicate the values of your business to the public? Who is the first person to show confidence, compassion, and competency to the people who walk in your door? It's the person who greets them. *That's* where your practice or business begins!"

Remember, earlier in the book, when I said, "Everything begins with 'hello' and 'you never get a second chance to give a first impression?'" I have put together five basic essentials that work in any industry for team building, effective communication when it comes to the goals of your company, and the art of being employee conscious.

RULE #1: EVERYBODY HAS TO SHOW UP

If you have created the kind of culture that stresses the perfect customer experience, everyone on your team understands that they have to come to work with an appropriate, positive attitude. That begins at the top—or the bottom, according to our inverted triangle—and extends upward to your employees. If they see you showing up with a smile on your face and a positive attitude, they will be inspired to show up.

RULE # 2: ENCOURAGE THE STAFF TO INSPIRE EACH OTHER

To effectively empower the team, *use* the team! Allow them to demonstrate ownership of the company, of the product, of the services, and they will go the extra mile for you, and this will, in turn, inspire the rest of your team. Encourage them to share their experience and their experiences with the rest of your team. Promote individuals in each department to become trainers and mentors to all new hires. These elite team members must walk the talk of your company's passion and core values. Managers, spend most of your time looking for opportunities to catch your team doing things exceptionally well instead of things poorly!

RULE #3: ENCOURAGE QUESTIONS, FEEDBACK, EVEN PUSHBACK

Inevitably, when you bring people together to brainstorm, you open up an arena where questions are welcome, where feedback is acknowledged, and where pushback is not only accepted but encouraged. An open dialogue has to be just that: open. You must insist that people leave judgment at the door. Questions, feedback, and pushback are meant to inspire and encourage, and who better to inspire and encourage than one's peers?

This is all about the team, and building a team is about mutual respect.

RULE #4: COMMUNICATE FROM THE HEART, BUT COACH BY THE BOOK

You've heard this one before or some variation on it. My interpretation goes something like this. Yes, you must have procedures and policies. Yes, you have to set goals and develop systems and strategies. And yes, your team must be empowered to act upon those strategies based on rules and regulations that support your business. However, if you consciously communicate these policies and procedures, goals and strategies, rules and regulations from a place in your heart, your employees will recognize your sincerity, and they will respond.

Here's the catch: You can't fake it. Communicating from your heart is only as good as the truth behind it. Your employees aren't dumb. They know sincerity when they see it, and they will respond accordingly.

RULE #5: INSPIRE YOUR STAFF WITH THE "MINT ON THE PILLOW"

Yes, I know we talked about this, but it bears repeating. When you create an atmosphere within your organization where people feel appreciated, needed, and, most importantly, respected, there is no telling how far you can go.

It's like the old saying: "People don't necessarily remember what you said to them, but they will always remember how you made them feel."

Yes, you want your team to go the extra mile for you and your organization, but they have to see that kind of behavior from you first. And you know what they respond to the most? It's the little things.

BE THE ONE WHO SETS THE BAR

Frankly, it's a great feeling to be the one who sets the bar rather than the person looking up at the bar. Whether it's overcoming a life-changing setback like I did as a kid or turning my company into a leader in service excellence, my goal is to set the highest standard. Be the team to beat. Be the one setting the pace and driving innovation, don't settle for second best! There's an energy and vitality in setting the bar, in being the leader, in asking "Why?" and "What if?"

Remember this, too: strategically, setting the bar offers the best vantage point of the future because, if you think about it, the front-runner has the most unobstructed view!

ACTION PLAN: SET THE BAR AND TURN YOUR DREAMS INTO REALITY

PLAN SMART:

Are you <u>specific</u> about where you're going? Can you <u>measure</u> what it will take to get there?

How do you know your goals are <u>achievable</u> and <u>realistic?</u> Have you set a clear <u>time limit</u> to accomplish everything?

START WITH THE "WHY?"

Do you have the courage to dig deep to get at the "why" beneath your dream? Can you write down "how" you will move forward in concrete ways? Then can you release all your energy and let your mind roam freely and creatively over the "What Ifs?"

LISTEN:

Do you take the time to let each customer/patient express themselves, and do you show your understanding and appreciation for their openness and vulnerability?

RESPOND:

Do you invite your customers/patients to contribute to the process by welcoming their good and bad feedback and responding to both their concerns and praise? Truthfully, the very same can be said when it comes to your employees.

TURN MISTAKES INTO OPPORTUNITIES:

Do you acknowledge mistakes and misunderstandings and clearly promise to make things not just right but even better than before? (e.g., send a gift certificate, make a call, write a note)

BE PERSONAL:

Are you consciously letting your customers/patients know they are valued in your eyes? Do <u>they</u> know that <u>you</u> know that <u>they</u> are the reason you are in business?! Make sure they do. As I like to verbally say to our patients /customers, "We are honored to have you in our ProGrin dental family. Please remember, I work for you; you don't work for me."

———

"Success Takes Time...Success Takes Effort!"

———

None of us—not you or me or the man on the moon—wants to look back on our life when we're old and grey and say, "I should have stepped out of the boat into unchartered waters and taken that chance, the chance that may have opened the door on that one special opportunity, the chance that would have allowed me to pursue my life-long goal, that chance that may well have propelled me to the life I always wanted to live."

We have talked about igniting the spark that propels you forward and drives you ever closer to your dreams. Sometimes that requires a heavy dose of tunnel vision. Sometimes it means blocking out everything and anything that might threaten your momentum and keep you from getting there.

It's a matter of mindset. Even when you feel like your world is crashing down around you, the one thing you control is your mindset. Your mindset is what you decide it can be. And if you choose not to give up, ever, then you're way ahead of the game. It's that simple.

I refuse to give up. Let's be honest. You'll never, ever be able to live with yourself if you give up, and no one wants to live with that regret.

We all must believe in ourselves and in our dreams, even when the masses don't. This is your dream, not theirs.

One thing I've found—and it's very comforting—is that striving for success and pursuing your dreams is a daily process. Igniting the spark that drives you toward success is a daily process. You can't shortchange the process. Get up every day and commit yourself to your dream.

Do we always know the answer? Of course not. Are we always a 100 percent sure of the direction we need to go? No. Are there times when we feel we've hit rock bottom? Most definitely. I say, embrace that. Embrace the down times and the pitfalls. Rock bottom doesn't rob you of your purpose or your desire. Rock bottom means the only direction you can go is UP!

Success takes time. Success takes effort! You've heard the saying, "Short-term sacrifices lead to long-term prosperity." I believe this to be true. I believe in taking short steps and tackling every obstacle head on. That's what makes the journey special.

There is another saying: "Living the Dash!" What "dash," you may ask? The dash following your birthday. In my case, it's July 29, 1955 —

That is exactly what I try to do every day. Live the dash fully and completely because, for now, there is no date following the dash. But one thing is certain: that dash following your birthdate will be smaller tomorrow than it is today. So don't waste another day!

Take action now. You are not guaranteed tomorrow!

Take that one small step toward achieving your dream, and then take another and another.

Today is the day. Now is the time.

Several years ago, I was watching the World Surfing Championship when a surfer grabbed the wave of a lifetime and set the world record for riding the highest wave for the longest duration. That's quite an accomplishment in the world of surfing.

After all the congratulations and high-fives, a reporter asked him, "Now that you've succeeded in reaching your dream of winning the World Championship and riding the biggest wave on record, what's next?"

The surfer didn't hesitate. He answered, "Tomorrow, when I wake up, I'll grab my surfboard, walk down to the beach, and **'paddle out.'** There's lots more waves to catch."

He could have said, "Well, I've achieved my dream. It's time to call it quits and hang up my board." But he didn't.

The lesson is simple. No matter the dream or the goal, it begins with one small step. It begins with taking action. Or, as they say in the world of surfing, paddle out!

I hope this book has inspired you to take the next step, never say never, and go after your dreams with passion!

On the next page, let me close by leaving you with two small but extremely powerful words…

what if

Dr. Ayers, Graduated from the Medical University of South Carolina College of Dental Medicine.

He has countless years of experience managing his own dental practices. Dr. Ayers, along with his son Brent co-founded ProGrin Dental and iGrin Pediatric Dentistry in 2012.

Dr. Ayers is also a teaching mentor at the acclaimed Nash Institute for Dental Learning. Aside from caring for his patients and mentoring doctors, Dr. Ayers co-authored the book *The Service Prescription- Health Care the Way it is Meant to be.*

He also enjoys dedicating his time to giving back to underprivileged communities and dental missions throughout Central and South America.

www.ingramcontent.com/pod-product-compliance
Lightning Source LLC
Chambersburg PA
CBHW070343220526
45467CB00001B/236